'Do not think the fairies are always little.
Everything about them is capricious, even their
size. They seem to take what size or shape
pleases them. Their chief occupations are feasting,
fighting, and making love, and playing
the most beautiful music. They have only one
industrious person amongst them, the *lepra-caun*,
the shoemaker. Perhaps they wear their shoes out
with dancing . . . And do they die? Blake saw a
fairy's funeral, but in Ireland we say they are
immortal.'

W. B. Yeats, from his Introduction to *Irish Fairy
and Folk Tales* (1893).

THE IRISH LEPRECHAUN'S KINGDOM

PETER HAINING

Designed by Christopher Scott

A PANTHER BOOK

GRANADA
London Toronto Sydney New York

For
OUR LITTLE PEOPLE
Philippa, Pamela,
Richard, Sean, Gemma, Jeremy and Nicholas.

Published by Granada Publishing Limited in 1981

ISBN 0 586 05323 9

First published in Great Britain by
Souvenir Press Ltd 1979
Copyright © Peter Haining and Pictorial Presentations 1979

Granada Publishing Limited
Frogmore, St. Albans, Herts AL2 2NF
and
3 Upper James Street, London W1R 4BP
866 United Nations Plaza, New York, NY10017, USA
117 York Street, Sydney, NSW 2000, Australia
100 Skyway Avenue, Rexdale, Ontario, M9W 3A6, Canada
PO Box 84165, Greenside, 2034 Johannesburg, South Africa
61 Beach Road, Auckland, New Zealand

Printed and bound in Great Britain by
William Clowes (Beccles) Limited,
Beccles and London
Set in Monophoto Times

Granada ®
Granada Publishing ®

CONTENTS

'The very tendency to superstition, so marked in Irish nature, arises from an instinctive dislike to the narrow limitations of common sense. It is characterised by a passionate yearning towards the vague, the mystic, the invisible, and the boundless infinite of the realms of imagination. Therefore the *Daoine Sidh*, the people of the fairy mansions, have an irresistible attraction for the Irish heart. Like them, the Irish love youth, beauty, splendour, lavish generosity, music and song, the feast and the dance. The mirth and reckless gaiety of the national temperament finds its true exponent in the mad pranks of the *Phouka* and the *Leprechaun*, the merry spirits that haunt the dells and glens, and look out at the wayfarer from under the dock-leaf with their glittering eyes. The inspiration that rises to poetry under the influence of excitement is expressed by the belief in the *Leanhaun Shee*, who gives power to song; while the deep pathos of Irish nature finds its fullest representation in the tender, plaintive, spiritual music of the wail and lamentation of the *Banshee*.'

Lady Wilde
ANCIENT LEGENDS OF IRELAND, 1888

INTRODUCTION

Ireland must surely be the very home of the supernatural.

For is it not a country where the gloom of day can make way suddenly for the bloodshot splendour of sunset? Where mist falls across the land in eerie veils, and clouds pile up like wraiths on the purple mountains? Where weird silences haunt the lonely hills and valleys and waves lap the rugged coastline with a melody unchanged since the ages long before the coming of man?

The Irish people, too, are quite unlike any other race. Surely no one else has such a keen appreciation of the supernatural, or is so aware that there is much in life no ordinary logic can explain? Nor perhaps are there any other folk so amply provided for with fables, so well stocked in myths, so rich in all manner of stories and legends.

Beyond all doubt, surely, Ireland is a place of the fantastic, and indeed its storytellers have celebrated the fact for two thousand years and more in oral traditions and folk stories which have been handed down lovingly with hardly a line changed. Tales that are full of the wonder of the place

(*Facing page*) 'The Last Gleeman' by J. B. Yeats for his son W. B. Yeat's book, *The Celtic Twilight* (1893). (*Above*) John D. Batten, the superb artist whose sketches were a feature of Joseph Jacob's two volumes of Celtic tales. This picture of King O'Toole was for *Celtic Fairy Tales* (1892).

and, more particularly, of the creatures which form the very heart and soul of this magic.

Though this book is called 'The Leprechaun's Kingdom' it is more, much more, than that. For the Leprechaun is only one of the spirits who flits through its pages – albeit the one best known and most widely associated with the country. This little manikin is one of a large and diverse band which includes such as the *Daoine Sidh*, the fairy host; the *Phouka*, that terrible steed of the night; and the ominous, wailing *Banshee*. To them we can add the grim, headless *Dullahans*; the *Far Darrigs*, those mischievous practical jokers; and the *Cluricaunes*, with their insatiable thirsts. Nor should we fail to mention the merrow (which we sometimes call mermaid), the changeling or fairy child, the water sheerie, and others of the pack like demons, ghosts, witches, werewolves and vampires, all of whom haunt the countryside as well as the minds of the people.

Such a multitude has naturally made the supernatural a particularly potent force in Ireland; a tradition cherished by the ordinary folk and an inspiration to writers and artists. And with this in mind, what I have set out to do in these pages is to represent this very special element of Irish life – this Celtic Wonderworld – in words and pictures.

The stories on which the very foundations of this magic world lie are from the people, of course: and it is these which the writers have utilised for their tales and the artists their models. For my part, as you will see, I have provided notes on each of our subjects and to these added the most revealing and interesting story about them I could find. The accompanying illustrations evoke the wonder probably even more strongly and are taken from many and diverse Irish sources.

The love and respect the Irish have always had for their mysterious little people – if I can use such a term to embrace all these creatures of the supernatural – has long been a source of amazement and even amusement to the rest of the world. And yet whenever I think of this aspect I am reminded of some words by the great Irish writer W. B. Yeats on the subject of 'Belief and Unbelief' in his book, *The Celtic Twilight* (1893) which seem to put the matter into a perspective it is almost impossible to deny.

'When all is said and done,' Mr Yeats wrote, 'how do we not know but that our own unreason may be better than another's truth? For it has been warmed on our hearths and in our souls, and is ready for the wild bees of truth to hive in it, and make their sweet honey. Come into the world again, wild bees, wild bees!'

APRIL 1979

MAN or WOMAN
BOY or GIRL
THAT READS WHAT
FOLLOWS
3 TIMES
SHALL FALL ASLEEP
AN HUNDRED YEARS

The Wailing Messenger of Death

The Banshee is one of Ireland's best known supernatural denizens – a midnight caller of doom which inspired the following famous lines:

> ' 'Twas the Banshee's lonely wailing
> Well I knew the voice of death,
> On the night wind slowly sailing
> O'er the bleak and gloomy heath.'

The *Bean Si*, as the spirit is correctly described, is 'The Lady of Death' who haunts very ancient Irish families. She appears just prior to a person's death and announces the fact by wailing and crying. The Banshee most usually appears within the vicinity of the ancestral home during the night hours, and although the voice is clearly that of a human female her lamentations are in a language that no one can understand. She may well come to the house several nights running before anyone dies, and it is possible the death forecast may be of someone who is staying elsewhere, even abroad. There are on record a number of instances of members of old Irish families dying thousands of miles away – as far as Canada and Australia – just as a Banshee is wailing outside their birthplace back in Ireland.

The Banshee materialises either as a beautiful young woman dressed in elegant garments such as a grey cloak and a green dress in the style of the Middle Ages, or else as a very old woman, bent and decrepit, enveloped in a winding-sheet or grave dress. Both types of *Bean Si* have long hair that streams in the wind and their eyes are fiery red from constant weeping. According to tradition the creature is very shy, easily irritated, and if annoyed will fly away and not return during the same generation. It is also believed that each Banshee is the spirit of a much earlier member of the same family who has been appointed as the messenger of death. Families of both high and low estate throughout Ireland are said to have their own Banshees, and the nation's folklore is replete with stories of their appearances. Perhaps the best known of them is the O'Neill's Banshee, a beautiful young woman who appears at

(*Facing page and below*) The two varieties of Bansee – the beautiful young woman and the old hag. Illustrations by H. R. Heaton for *Irish Wonders* by D. R. McAnally (1888).

SONG OF THE BANSHEE.

the family's home, Shane's Castle by Lough Neagh. The sixteenth-century castle was the stronghold of Shane O'Neill, and when the *Bean Si* appears to sing her lament of death she is said to pace through the actual rooms of the building as well as walking outside.

The Banshee is also associated with three other spirit forms. The first of these is *Babd,* the Irish goddess of battles, a species of *valkyrie,* who haunts battlefields, sometimes in the shape of a raven, picking at the bodies of the dead with her beak. The second is *Morrigan,* a nightmare figure, capable of changing her form to beguile the unwary. And finally the *Bean-Nighe,* a pale, slender woman seen washing blood-stained garments in the waters of a river and by so doing prophesying death in battle.

Stories of Banshees apparently particularly fascinated the first great collector of Irish folklore, Thomas Crofton Croker (1798–1854), who quoted several examples in his work, *Fairy Legends and Traditions of the South of Ireland* (1825–8) including one of which he had personal experience! He wrote:

'An instance of this superstition occurred in the writer's family. A servant, named Peggy Rilehan, declared that some great misfortune was about to happen, as she had heard a shriek, and had seen something pass across the window: On this the writer's sister, who was present at the time, remarks – "I saw nothing, but I heard Peggy scream, and then exclaim – 'There it is – there it is – what always appears when any of the Rilehans are to die.'" She says she saw it before, when aunt Harriott's nurse (who was her grandmother) died at Mallow. The poor girl's cousin was at this time in jail. He was one of the misguided followers of Captain Rock; and two or three days after was tried for being concerned in the attack on Churchtown barrack, found guilty and executed.'

Croker thought one of the most interesting cases of an Irish Banshee was that quoted by Sir Walter Scott in his *The Lady of the Lake* (1810). It appeared as a footnote, yet Croker thought it 'too curious to be omitted' from his collection and included it as follows on the facing page.

(*Above*) 'The Banshee of the MacCarthys' by T. Crofton Croker – a famous story of this supernatural creature illustrated by James Torrance for *Irish Folk and Fairy Tales* by W. B. Yeats (1893).
(*Below*) The traditional Irish idea of the Banshee as pictured in *Fairy Legends and Traditions of the South of Ireland* by T. Crofton Croker (1825–8).

'The Banshee Appears' a picture by R. Prowse for a serial story, 'The Whiteboys' in *The Halfpenny Miscellany* (1862).

The Face at the Window

HE most remarkable instance of the appearance of a Banshee occurs in the MS Memoirs of Lady Fanshaw, so exemplary for her conjugal affection. Her husband, Sir Richard, and she chanced, during their abode in Ireland, to visit a friend, the head of a sept, who resided in an ancient baronial castle, surrounded with a moat.

At midnight she was awakened by a ghastly and supernatural scream and, looking out of bed, beheld, by the moonlight, a female face and part of the form hovering at the window. The distance from the ground, as well as the circumstance of the moat, excluded the possibility that what she beheld was of this world.

The face was that of a young and rather handsome woman, but pale, and the hair, which was reddish, loose and dishevelled. The dress, which Lady Fanshaw's terror did not prevent her remarking accurately, was that of the ancient Irish.

This apparition continued to exhibit itself for some time, and then vanished, with two shrieks similar to that which had first excited Lady Fanshaw's attention.

In the morning, with infinite terror, she communicated to her host what she had witnessed, and found him prepared not only to credit, but to account for the apparition.

'A near relation of my family,' he explained, 'expired last night in this castle. We disguised our certain expectation of the event from you, lest it should throw a cloud over the cheerful reception which was your due. Now, before such an event happens in this family and castle, the female spectre whom you have seen is always visible. She is believed to be the spirit of a woman of inferior rank, whom one of my ancestors degraded himself by marrying, and whom afterwards, to expiate the dishonour done to his family, he caused to be drowned in the Castle moat.'

Lady Fanshaw lived in turbulent and unsettled times, when to the lively imagination every sight and sound came fraught with dismal forebodings of evil. Perhaps this reasoning will account for the Banshee being a spirit so familiar in Ireland.

The Ancient Spirits of the coast

The first two races of people to settle in Ireland were the *Firbolgs* and the *Tuatha de Dannan*, and it is from them that the Cave Fairies evolved, who now live in the shallow waters and inlets all around the coast.

The *Firbolgs* apparently first came to Ireland at some period lost in the mists of time and were large, grotesque creatures. Despite their strength, however, they proved no match for the *Tuatha de Dannan*, the people of the Goddess Diana, who arrived later on the scene and drove them off after a series of bloody battles. In hiding, the stature of the *Firbolgs*

CAVE FAIRIES

degenerated until they were no more than three feet high with dark complexions and thick, pot-bellied stomachs. They did, however, develop the power to change their shape and take on human form if they so desired. Today they are said to dress in peasant costumes and be generally helpful to mankind.

The *Tuatha de Dannan*, who also ruled over Ireland until they, too, were conquered by new invaders, the Milesians, did have a rather more profound effect on the life of the country in cultural terms. However, they also became fairy people after their banishment, and eventually evolved into the *Daoine Sidh*, or 'Good People' as we know them today.

On page 18 another early collector of Irish folklore, Lady Jane Wilde (1826–96), the mother of Oscar Wilde, and a distinguished author in her own right under the name of 'Speranza', recounts the legend of the *Tuatha de Dannan* in an extract from her major work, *Ancient Legends of Ireland* (1888).

(*Facing page*) The Cave Fairy – a picture from *Folk and Fairy Tales* by Mrs Burton Harrison (1885).
(*Above*) The Firbolgs as imagined in an anonymous collection of *Irish Legends* (1884).

(*Left*) John D. Batten's idea of the Cave Fairies today for *More Celtic Fairy Tales* by John Jacobs (1894). (*Facing page*) The *Tuatha de Dannan* eventually declined into the *Daoine Sidh* – a picture by Stephen Reid for *Myths and Legends of the Celtic Race* by T. W. Rolleston (1912).

The Magic People

T is believed by many people that the cave fairies are the remnant of the ancient *Tuatha-de-Dannans* who once ruled Ireland, but were conquered by the Milesians.

These *Tuatha* were great necromancers, skilled in all magic, and excellent in all the arts as builders, poets, and musicians. At first the Milesians were going to destroy them utterly, but gradually were so fascinated and captivated by the gifts and power of the *Tuatha* that they allowed them to remain and to build forts, where they held high festival with music and singing and the chant of the bards.

And the breed of horses they reared could not be surpassed in the world – fleet as the wind, with the arched neck and the broad chest and the quivering nostril, and the large eye that showed they were made of fire and flame, and not of dull, heavy earth. The *Tuatha* made stables for them in the great caves of the hills, and they were shod with silver and had golden bridles, and never a slave was allowed to ride them.

A splendid sight was the cavalcade of the *Tuatha-de-Dannan* knights. Seven-score steeds, each with a jewel on his forehead like a star, and seven-score horsemen, all the sons of kings, in their green mantles fringed with gold, and golden helmets on their heads, and golden greaves on their limbs, and each knight having in his hand a golden spear.

But soon after the power of the *Tuatha-de-Dannan* was broken for ever, and the remnant that was left took refuge in the caves where they exist to this day, and practise their magic, and work spells, and are safe from death until the judgment day.

Sometimes the cave fairies make a straight path in the sea from one is-land to another, all paved with coral, under the water; but no one can tread it except the fairy race. Fishermen coming home late at night, on looking down, have frequently seen them passing and re-passing – a black band of little men with black dogs, who are very fierce if any one tries to touch them.

There was an old man named Con, who lived on an island all alone, except for a black dog who kept him company. Now all the people knew right well that he was a fairy king, and could walk the water at night like the other fairies. So they feared him greatly, and brought him presents of cakes and fowls, for they were afraid of him and of his evil demon, the dog. For often, men coming home late have heard the steps of this dog and his breathing quite close to them, though they could not see him; and one man nearly died of fright, and was only saved by the priest who came and prayed over him.

Children of the Fairies

The idea that fairies steal away babies and small children and leave changelings in their place is a very old tradition in Ireland. Indeed it is a very widespread belief and both Shakespeare (in *Midsummer Night's Dream*, Act 2, scene 1) and Spenser (*Faerie Queene*, Book 1, canto 10) mention it in their work, the latter writing:

'A Fairy thee unweeting reft,
There as thou slept in tender swadling band,
And her base elfin brood there for thee left,
Such men do changelings call – so changed by fairies theft.'

The changelings can be actual fairy children, but are more likely to be old, possibly senile fairies, disguised as children. Sometimes they can even be an inanimate object such as a log of wood bewitched so that it seems to be human.

For many centuries in Ireland the parents of ugly, deformed or moronic children were often comforted with the thought that the baby was not their own, but a substitute left by fairies after the original had been spirited away to fairy-land. A number of tests were devised to establish whether or not a child was a changeling, the most infallible said to be to lay it on a shovel over the fire repeating the words, 'Burn, burn, burn – if of the Devil, burn; but if of God and the saints, be safe from harm.' If the child was a changeling it would immediately rush up the chimney for, as one authority has put it, 'fire is the greatest of enemies to every sort of phantom, in so much that those who have seen apparitions fall into a swoon as they are sensible of the brightness of fire'. Instances of this test being applied to children have been reported right into the present century in parts of Ireland. Another method which is suggested is to beat the child until its screams of pain and fright bring back the fairies to reclaim it. Less horrible than either of these is the belief that a changeling could be made to reveal its identity by crossing it over a stream (they hate water) or by trying to make it laugh (they are only joyful when something evil happens).

According to Irish tradition any child that is not baptised or is admired too much runs the risk of being carried off by the fairies, and the way to ensure protection against this is to hang a pair of scissors over the infant's bed or lay an article of its father's clothing over it while it sleeps.

The story 'The Brewery of Egg-Shells' is one of the most famous about changelings and is taken from T. Crofton Croker's collection.

CHANGELINGS

(*Facing page*) Superb illustration of fairies stealing a human baby and replacing it with one of their own. This picture was by Michael Ayrton for *Myths and Traditions* (1952). (*Right*) An Arthur Rackham illustration of 'The Changeling' with a group of beautiful fairies.

The Brewery of Egg-shells

 OW Mrs Sullivan fancied that her youngest child had been changed by 'fairies theft', and certainly appearances warranted such a conclusion; for in one night her healthy, blue-eyed boy had become shrivelled up into almost nothing, and never ceased squalling and crying. This naturally made poor Mrs Sullivan very unhappy; and all the neighbours, by way of comforting her, said that her own child was, beyond any kind of doubt, with the good people, and that one of themselves was put in his place.

Mrs Sullivan of course could not disbelieve what every one told her, but she did not wish to hurt the thing; for although its face was so withered, and its body wasted away to a mere skeleton, it had still a strong resemblance to her own boy. She therefore could not find it in her hear to roast it alive on the griddle, or to burn its nose off with the red-hot tongs, or to throw it out in the snow on the road-side, notwithstanding these, and several like proceedings, were strongly recommended to her for the recovery of her child.

One day who should Mrs Sullivan meet but a cunning woman, well known about the country by the name of Ellen Leah (or Grey Ellen). She had the gift, however she got it, of telling where the dead were, and what was good for the rest of their souls; and could charm away warts and wens, and do a great many wonderful things of the same nature.

'You're in grief this morning, Mrs Sullivan,' were the first words of Ellen Leah to her.

'You may say that, Ellen,' said Mrs Sullivan, 'and good cause I have to be in grief, for there was my own fine child whipped off from me out of his cradle, without as much as by your leave or ask your pardon, and an ugly dony bit of a shrivelled up fairy put in his place; no wonder then that you see me in grief, Ellen.'

'Small blame to you, Mrs Sullivan,' said Ellen Leah; 'but are you sure 'tis a fairy?'

(*Above*) John D. Batten illustration for 'The Brewery of Egg-shells' in Jacob's *Celtic Fairy Tales*.

'Sure!' echoed Mrs Sullivan, 'sure enough am I to my sorrow, and can I doubt my own two eyes? Every mother's soul must feel for me!'

'Will you take an old woman's advice?' said Ellen Leah, fixing her wild and mysterious gaze upon the unhappy mother; and, after a pause, she added, 'but may be you'll call it foolish?'

'Can you get me back my child, my own child, Ellen?' said Mrs Sullivan with great energy.

'If you do as I bid you,' returned Ellen Leah, 'you'll know.' Mrs Sullivan was silent in expectation, and Ellen continued, 'Put down the big pot, full of water, on the fire, and make it boil like mad; then get a dozen new-laid eggs, break them, and keep the shells, but throw away the rest; when that is done, put the shells in the pot of boiling water, and you will soon know whether it is

your own boy or a fairy. If you find that it is a fairy in the cradle, take the red-hot poker and cram it down his ugly throat, and you will not have much trouble with him after that, I promise you.'

Home went Mrs Sullivan, and did as Ellen Leah desired. She put the pot on the fire, and plenty of turf under it, and set the water boiling at such a rate, that if ever water was red-hot, it surely was.

The child was lying for a wonder quite easy and quiet in the cradle, every now and then cocking his eye, that would twinkle as keen as a star in a frosty night, over at the great fire, and the big pot upon it; and he looked on with great attention at Mrs Sullivan breaking the eggs, and putting down the egg-shells to boil. At last he asked, with the voice of a very old man, 'What are you doing, mammy?'

Mrs Sullivan's heart, as she said herself, was up in her mouth ready to choke her, at hearing the child speak. But she contrived to put the poker in the fire, and to answer without making any wonder at the words, 'I'm brewing, *a vick*' (my son).

(*Above*) A mother and fairies battle over a human baby. A picture by T. H. Thomas for *British Goblins* by Wirt Sikes (1880).

'And what are you brewing, mammy?' said the little imp, whose supernatural gift of speech now proved beyond question that he was a fairy substitute.

'I wish the poker was red,' thought Mrs Sullivan; but it was a large one, and took a long time heating: so she determined to keep him in talk until the poker was in a proper state to thrust down his throat, and therefore repeated the question.

'Is it what I'm brewing, *a vick*,' said she, 'you want to know?'

'Yes, mammy: what are you brewing?' returned the fairy.

'Egg-shells, *a vick*,' said Mrs Sullivan.

'Oh!' shrieked the imp, starting up in the cradle, and clapping his hands together, 'I'm fifteen hundred years in the world, and I never saw a brewery of egg-shells before!' The poker was by this time quite red, and Mrs Sullivan seizing it ran furiously towards the cradle; but somehow or other her foot slipped, and she fell flat on the floor, and the poker flew out of her hand to the other end of the house. However, she got up without much loss of time and went to the cradle, intending to pitch the wicked thing that was in it into the pot of boiling water, when there she saw her own child in a sweet sleep, one of his soft round arms rested upon the pillow – his features were as placid as if their repose had never been disturbed, save the rosy mouth, which moved with a gentle and regular breathing.

Who can tell the feelings of a mother when she looks upon her sleeping child? Why should I therefore endeavour to describe those of Mrs Sullivan at again beholding her long-lost boy? The fountains of her heart overflowed with the excess of joy, and she wept! – tears trickled silently down her cheek, nor did she strive to check them – they were tears not of sorrow, but of happiness.

(*Above*) The Cluricaune by John D. Batten for *Celtic Fairy Tales*.
(*Left and far right*) Two illustrations of the mischievous Cluricaune at his pranks from the Brothers Grimm translation of Crofton Croker's work, *Irische Elfenmarchen*.

The Mischievous Little Drinker

The *Cluricaune* is one of the trio of Ireland's best known solitary fairies – the others are the *Leprechaun* and the *Far Darrig* – all of them preferring their own company rather than congregating in groups. This particular fairy is an old, withered little man who delights in spending his time getting drunk in wine cellars! Not surprisingly the word *Naggeneen* is sometimes given to him, which implies a small measure of drink – and the term is roughly equivalent to the English word 'noggin', another measure about the same as a gill.

Although the *Cluricaune* has no compunction about helping himself to the household wine and beer, he is also said to scare off anyone else, including servants, who help themselves without the master's permission. Though whether this is to protect his own interests is anyone's guess! There are a number of accounts in Irish folklore of these creatures making such nuisances of themselves, and drinking such large quantities of wine, that the families being plagued by them have been forced to move house. But such people have had to make quite sure that the mischievous little drinker has not popped into one of the wine barrels and hidden himself there for the removal!

Aside from his intemperate habits, this little man always dresses well – wearing a red coat and tall cap, a leather apron, long, pale-blue stockings and high-heeled shoes with silver-buckles. He is also said to like a *Dudeen*, a small stumpy pipe of tobacco. Some legends say he knows where hidden treasure is buried, and he possesses a little leather purse known as the *Sprè na Skillenagh*, or Shilling Fortune, which contains a coin to this value, and no matter how often it is spent always replaces itself.

Understandably no doubt, the *Cluricaune* is not well thought of in Ireland, and although many people have tried to outwit them, they are adept at using their cunning and avaricious natures to turn the tables on poor mankind. Even when trapped, it is said, they still have the ability to turn themselves invisible and make good their escape.

The story on the next page of a particularly troublesome member of the clan was again collected by T. Crofton Croker.

CLURICAUNES

Wildbeam's Pranks

R HARRIS, a quaker, had a Cluricaune in his family: it was very diminutive in form. If any of the servants, as they sometimes do through negligence, left the beer barrel running, little Wildbeam (for that was his name) would wedge himself into the cock and stop it at the risk of being smothered, until some one came to turn the key. In return for such services, the cook was in the habit, by her master's orders, of leaving a good dinner in the cellar for little Wildbeam.

One Friday it so happened that she had nothing to leave but part of a herring and some cold potatoes, when just at midnight something pulled her out of bed, and having brought her with irresistible force to the top of the cellar stairs, she was seized by the heels and dragged down them; at every knock her head received against the stairs, the Cluricaune, who was standing at the door, would shout out –

'Molly Jones – Molly Jones –
Potato-skins and herring-bones!
I'll knock your head against the stones!
Molly Jones – Molly Jones.'

The poor cook was so much bruised by that night's adventure, she was confined to her bed for three weeks after. In consequence of this piece of violent conduct, Mr Harris wished much to get rid of his fairy attendant; and being told if he removed to any house beyond a running stream, that the Cluricaune could not follow him, he took a house, and had all his furniture packed on carts for the purpose of removing: the last articles brought out were the cellar furniture; and when the cart was completely loaded with casks and barrels, the Cluricaune was seen to jump into it, and fixing himself in the bunghole of an empty cask, cried out to Mr Harris, 'Here, master! here we go, all together!'

'What!' said Mr Harris, 'dost thou go also?'

'Yes, to be sure, master,' replied little Wildbeam; 'here we go, all together.'

'In that case, friend,' said Mr Harris, 'let the carts be unpacked; we are just as well where we are.'

Mr Harris died soon after, but it is said the Cluricaune still attends the Harris family.

Mr. Harris' Cluricaune, 'Wildbeam' – a picture from Crofton Croker's *Fairy Legends*.

(*Right*) Another of John D. Batten's whimsical pictures for Jacobs' *More Celtic Fairy Tales*.
(*Below*) Mischief surprised – a delightful sketch by W. H. Brooke for J. Keightley's story of Cluricaunes in his book, *Fairy Mythology* (1880).

The Immortal Fairy Folk

The *Daoine Sidh* – or just simple *Sidhe* – are the 'Good People', the fairy folk of Ireland. The Irish word for fairy is *sheehogue*, a diminutive of shee in banshee, and this provides another expression for fairy people, the *deenee shee*.

There are two major schools of thought as to how these remarkable creatures originated. On the one hand they are said to be the dwindled folk of the *Tuatha de Dannan*, those early settlers of Ireland. While another tradition says they are fallen angels 'not good enough to be saved, nor bad enough to be lost' to quote an old saying. Followers of the first school will cite as evidence the fact that many fairy chiefs have the same names as the old *Tuatha* heroes, and that they have the habit of meeting on the burial-grounds of that ancient race. As to their being fallen angels, evidence is offered as to their mischievous nature, their habit of repaying evil with evil, good for good, and their desire to be regarded with respect and have offerings made to them.

In introducing his *Irish Fairy and Folk Tales* (1893), W. B. Yeats (1865–1939) has given us a good picture of them: 'Do not think the fairies are always little. Everything is capricious about them, even their size. They seem to take what size or shape pleases them. Their chief occupations are feasting, fighting, and making love, and playing the most beautiful music. They have only one industrious person amongst them, the *lepra-caun*, the shoemaker. Perhaps they wear their shoes out with dancing.' Mr Yeats says they have three great festivals of the year: May Eve for fighting, Midsummer Eve when they are gayest, and November Eve when they mourn the coming of winter and dance with ghosts. They have their own palaces, or *raths*, where they gather for these revels. He also reports that their singing has the power to bewitch any listener, and if they are provoked to anger they have fairy darts which can paralyse men or cattle. 'And do they die?' he asks finally, 'Blake saw a fairy's funeral, but in Ireland we say they are immortal.'

The following story of one man's experiences with the fairy people is from another early and important book of folklore, *Legendary Fictions of the Irish Celts* Collected by Patrick Kennedy (1866).

DAOINE SIDH

(*Facing page*) A group of fairy folk at their midnight revels – an engraving by Gustave Doré (1875).
(*Left*) A delighted observer watches fairies dancing around their Queen. A picture by W. H. Brooke for Keightley's *Fairy Mythology*.

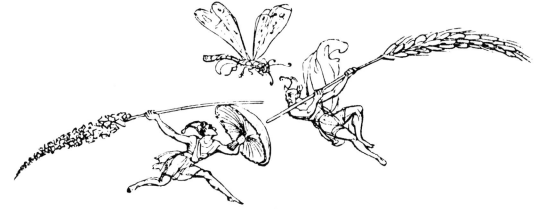

A selection of illustrations of fairy revels from Crofton Croker's famous book, *Fairy Legends*. Although the artist is uncredited, it is believed to have been George Maclise. (*Facing page: top*) An unsuspecting human tempted to drink a fairy brew. Picture by T. H. Thomas for *British Goblins* by Wirt Sikes. (*Bottom*) Another Thomas illustration of two men being tempted by the fairies to join in their dancing, from *British Goblins*.

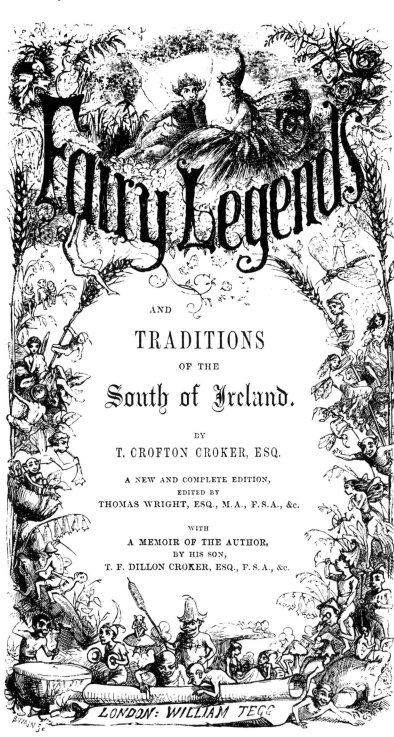

Fairy Legends

AND

TRADITIONS

OF THE

South of Ireland.

BY

T. CROFTON CROKER, ESQ.

A NEW AND COMPLETE EDITION,
EDITED BY
THOMAS WRIGHT, ESQ., M.A., F.S.A., &c.

WITH

A MEMOIR OF THE AUTHOR,
BY HIS SON,
T. F. DILLON CROKER, ESQ., F.S.A., &c.

LONDON: WILLIAM TEGG

Jemmy Doyle in the Fairy Palace

Y father was once coming down Scollagh Gap on a dark night, and all at once he saw, right before him, the lights coming from ever so many windows of a castle, and heard the shouts and laughing of people within. The door was wide open, and in he walked; and there on the spot where he had often drunk a tumbler of bad beer, he found himself in a big hall, and saw the king and queen of the fairies sitting at the head of a long table, and hundreds of people, all grandly dressed, eating and drinking. The clothes they had on them were of an old fashion, and there were harpers and pipers by themselves up in a gallery, and playing the most delightful old Irish airs. There was nothing to be seen but rich silk dresses, and

pearls, and diamonds on the gentlemen and ladies, and rich hangings on the walls, and lamps blazing.

The queen, as soon as she saw my father, cried out, 'Welcome, Mr Doyle; make room there for Mr Doyle, and let him have the best at the table. Hand Mr Doyle a tumbler of punch, that will be strong and sweet. Sit down, Mr Doyle, and make yourself welcome.' So he sat down, and took the tumbler, and just as he was going to taste it, his eye fell on the man next him, and he was an old neighbour that was dead twenty years. Says the old neighbour, 'For your life, don't touch it nor sup.' The smell was very nice, but he was frightened by what the dead neighbour said, and he began to notice how ghastly some of the fine people looked when they thought he was not minding them.

So his health was drunk, and he was pressed by the queen to fall to, but he had the sense to take the neighbour's advice, and only spilled the drink down between his coat and waistcoat.

At last the queen called for a song, and one of the guests sang a very indecent one in Irish. He often repeated a verse of it for us, but we

didn't know the sense. At last he got sleepy, and recollected nothing more only the rubbing of his legs against the bushes in the knoc (field of gorse) above our place in Cromogue; and we found him asleep next morning in the haggard, with a scent of punch from his mouth. He told us that we would get his knee-buckles on the path at the upper end of the knoc, and there, sure enough, they were found. Heaven be his bed!

(*Facing page: far left*) Fairy Music from *More Celtic Fairy Tales* and (*Above*) 'The Fairy Dance' by Gustave Doré (1875). (*Left*) James Torrance illustration for 'A Donegal Fairy' by Letitia Maclintock and (*this page*) another of his pictures for 'Frank Martin and The Fairies' by William Carleton. Both are from *Irish Fairy and Folk Tales*.

(*Above*) 'The Dark of the Sea' an illustration by John D. Batten for *More Celtic Fairy Tales*. (*Below*) Fanciful interpretation of the Fomorians by W. H. Brooke for Keightley's *Fairy Mythology*. (*Facing page*) A Fomorian based on *The Book of the Dun Cow* and drawn by John D. Batten.

The Dark of the Sea

Ireland has its own particular kind of demons, the Fomorians, who, according to legend, have been living off the coast of Donegal since the very earliest times. They are hideous, evil creatures, whose name means 'the dark of the sea', and it is believed they actually dwell in an underwater city known as Lochlan.

Such is their importance in local folklore that in a very ancient Irish manuscript, *The Book of the Dun Cow* (*c.* 1090), they are given an entire chapter entitled 'The History of Monsters or the Fomorians and Dwarfs'. In this they are described as having the bodies of men and heads like those of goats, although they can adopt a variety of other appearances. In the years of pre-history they attacked and enslaved as many of the races of Irish settlers as they could, until finally one group known as the Nemed defeated them in a terrible battle in which the king of the Fomorians, Conann, was killed. Thereafter they retreated into their underwater stronghold and have been little heard of since.

The most famous of the Fomorians was Balor of the Evil Eye who was said to be able to kill a person with a single glance of one of his eyes. Indeed fear of the Evil Eye among the Irish may well have originated from this demon, and it is a fact of life that has long been recorded as Lady Wilde has written: 'Nothing is more dreaded by the peasantry than the full, fixed, direct glance of one suspected of the Evil Eye, and should it fall upon them, or on any of their household, a terrible fear and trembling of heart takes possession of them, which often ends in sickness or sometimes even in death.' Lady Wilde herself included the legend of Balor in her collection as given next.

DEMONS

The Fomorian King, Conann, rides
into battle: an old eighteenth-century
engraving.

The Evil Eye

 HE influence of the mysterious and malign power of the Evil Eye has at all times been as much dreaded in Ireland as it is in Egypt, Greece, or Italy at the present day. Everything young beautiful, or perfect after its kind, and which naturally attracts attention and admiration, is peculiarly liable to the fatal blight that follows the glance of the Evil Eye. It is therefore an invariable habit among the peasantry never to praise anything without instantly adding, 'God bless it'; for were this formula omitted, the worse consequences would befall the object praised.

The superstition must be of great antiquity in Ireland, for Balor, the Fomorian giant and hero, is spoken of in an ancient manuscript as able to petrify his enemies by a glance; and how he became possessed of the power is thus narrated.

One day as the Druids were busy at their incantations, while boiling a magical spell or charm, young Balor passed by, and curious to see their work, looked in at an open window. At that moment the Druids happened to raise the lid of the caldron, and the vapour, escaping, passed under one of Balor's eyes, carrying with it all the venom of the incantation. This caused his brow to grow to such a size that it required four men to raise it whenever he wanted to exert the power of his venomed glance over his enemies. He was slain at last in single combat, according to the ancient legend, at the great battle of Magh-Tura (the plain of the towers), fought between the *Firbolgs* and the *Tuatha-de-Dananns* for the possession of Ireland several centuries before the Christian era; for before Balor's brow could be lifted so that he could transfix his enemy and strike him dead with the terrible power of his glance, his adversary flung a stone with such violence that it went right through the Evil Eye, and pierced the skull, and the mighty magician fell to rise no more.

(*Left*) Balor of The Evil Eye – a picture by John D. Batten.
(*Below*) A Fomorian with the head of a goat, from an eighteenth-century history of Ireland.

(*Above*) The bizarre, headless Dullahans as pictured in Crofton Croker's *Fairy Legends*.
(*Facing page*) Engraving for the story of 'The Elfin Piper' in *Tales of Fairy Land* (1847).

The Ride of the Headless Phantom

Although headless ghosts are by no means peculiar to Ireland, the country can boast a most unusual variety in the *Dullahan*, or *Dubhlachan* as it is sometimes called. According to experts, the word *Dubhlachan* originally signified a dark, sullen person, but over the centuries it has become applied to this unusual phantom.

The particular function of the *Dullahans* is to drive the Death Coach, or *Coach a bower*, which appears at midnight. When it gallops up to any particular house and the coachman's whip can be heard cracking loudly then this is said to be an omen that someone within the house is going to die shortly. In his book of legends, T. Crofton Croker quotes the following account of the *Dullahans* which was sent to him by a lady living in Cork:

'They drive particularly hard wherever a death is going to take place. The people about here thought that the road would be completely worn out with their galloping before Mrs Spiers died. On the night the poor lady departed they brought an immense procession with them, and instead of going up the road as usual, they turned into Tivoli: the lodge-people, according to their own account, "were *kilt* from them that night". The coachman has a most marvellously long whip, with which he can whip the eyes out of anyone, at any distance, that dares to look at him. I suppose the reason he is so incensed at being looked at, is because he cannot return the compliment, *'pon the 'count* of having no head. What a pity it is none but the *Dullahans* can go without their heads! Some people's heads would be no less to them, or any one else.'

Perhaps the two best known examples of the Dullahans are the headless phantom that used to stand in Sligo streets on dark nights, and the black coach drawn by headless horses which drives through the town of Doneraile, stopping at the doors of different houses. Anyone foolish enough to look out on it, has a basin of blood thrown instantly in their face!

The following story of a Dullahan comes from the town of Timogue in Queen's County and is related by Canon John O'Hanlon who, under the pen-name 'Lageniensis', collected a good deal of important folklore and published it in *Irish Local Legends* (1896).

DULLAHANS

The Death Coach

THERE can be no question but that historical and traditional stories are strangely woven together, and with many tangles of net-work, in the fireside narratives of our peasantry. These regarding Timogue old church, and the castle which formerly stood near it, are examples of fact and fiction, it should prove difficult at present to unravel. Although of comparatively modern erection and architecturally of a debased style, the church seems to rise on the ruins of an earlier structure; for on the exterior, the grass-covered graves, and rude heading stones, noteless of inscriptions, rise nearly to the sills of the windows, owing to the accumulation of mouldering human remains that have been deposited under earth, so frequently re-opened in the well-known family burial plots, for centuries long past. Those first entombed there are unrecorded in documents, and not remembered in traditions. All over the cemetery – a popular place for interments – flag-tombs, half hidden in the mould, or head-stones sinking deeper into it each year, are interspersed with the furrows showing where the latest graves had been opened and sodded over, while crowned with a luxurious crop of grass and weeds. Solitude has settled round the site by day; and night adds to it a still deeper gloom.

Late in the last century, the trade in wool was very considerable in the midland counties of Ireland, and a revival of home manufactures caused a brisk demand for fleeces, which were brought in packs by the shepherd farmers to certain established fairs for sale. On one of those occasions, a wool-comber and his driver of the cart, on which the well-stuffed wool-packs had been placed, were returning from the fair of Ballynakill, and rather belated, they were approaching the old graveyard of Timogue, which was observed on their right with the high wall surrounding it on the roadside. The night was dark and stormy; the witching hour for goblins stalking abroad had come; nor was it pleasant to trudge the miry way; when suddenly, a blaze of fire shot up from the graveyard within the wall, in which a breach seemed to yawn wider each moment, until at length it opened for several yards. Then followed a loud rumbling noise, while a black coach, with a coachman and four headless horses, was observed rolling out towards the road, to the horror of the unprotected travellers. Nevertheless, as the urgency of fear was uppermost, and as flight towards the bridge and their homeward-bound course was instinctive, the driver and his master jumped on the cart, the former raised his whip, and the horse, in like manner seized with terror, bounded forward. Nearer and nearer the unearthly equipage seemed to gain upon them; louder and louder arose the rearward clattering of hoofs and the rolling of wheels. Petrified with fright, the fugitives ventured to look behind, and they beheld one of the most diabolical countenances it could be possible to imagine looking out of the coach, and with a mouth grinning from ear to ear, as if gloating over the idea of seizing the fugitives.

Agonised beyond endurance at this awful spectacle, the driver and his companion screamed out with all their might; but they had already reached the crowning arch of the

bridge, where the water beneath proved to be their safeguard, and a barrier over which the demon coach could not pass. Suddenly it stopped short; then turned back; by degrees, the sounds of horses' feet and rolling wheels grew fainter, as that apparition vanished in the distance. Such was the story as narrated to the writer, now many long years ago.

(*Facing page*) A phantom carriage and pair. (*Above*) A headless ghost from *The Idler* (1893).

The RedMan's Pranks

The *Far Darrig* is a practical joker who particularly loves gruesome pranks, and he has many traits in common with the English Hob-Goblin and the German Kobold. Stories of his mischief are told all over Ireland, but in strange contrast it is said he also loves cleanliness and things kept well ordered! Unlike many other spirits he attaches himself to a house or a locality rather than a family.

The expression *Far Darrig*, or *Fear Dearg* as it is sometimes spelt, means Red Man, and the little creature invariably dresses in a red cap and coat. He is celebrated in the old verse:

'Ned! Ned!
By my cap so red!
You're as good, Ned,
As a man that is dead!'

T. Crofton Croker in his *Fairy Legends and Traditions of the South of Ireland* gives us an interesting pen portrait of the creature: 'The red dress and strange flexibility of voice possessed by the *Far Darrig* form his peculiar characteristics; the latter is said, by Irish tale-tellers, to be as *Fuaim na dtonn*, the sound of waves; and again, it is compared to *Ceol na naingeal*, the music of angels; *Ceileabhar na nèan*, the warbling of birds, &c; and the usual address to this fairy is, *Na dean fochmoid fàinn*, do not mock us. His entire dress, when he is seen, is invariably described as crimson.'

In certain old Irish traditions the *Far Darrig* has been known to help human beings trapped in Fairyland to escape, while in others he is said to have the ability to appear as 'a gigantic fellow'. Perhaps the best known of these creatures was the *Fear Dearg* of Munster, a little old man with long grey hair and wrinkled face, about two and a half foot high, who wore a scarlet sugar-loaf hat and long scarlet cloak. It was his practice to request permission to warm himself at people's fires and dire misfortune would fall on anyone who refused.

The best known story of a *Far Darrig* is the following example by the Irish storyteller, Letitia Maclintock, which was reprinted several times after its first appearance in the 1890s, but has been unavailable for much of this century.

(*Facing page*) Gruesome illustration by James Torrance for Letitia Maclintock's story of the 'Far Darrig in Donegal'. (*Above, left*) A Far Darrig at his practical jokes in Keightley's *Fairy Mythology* illustrated by W. H. Brooke.

Far Darrig in Donegal

AT DIVER, the tinker, was a man well-accustomed to a wandering life, and to strange shelters; he had shared the beggar's blanket in smoky cabins; he had crouched beside the still in many a nook and corner where poteen was made on the wild Innishowen mountains; he had even slept on the bare heather, or on the ditch, with no roof over him but the vault of heaven; yet were all his nights of adventure tame and commonplace when compared with one especial night.

During the day preceding that night, he had mended all the kettles and saucepans in Moville and Greencastle, and was on his way to Culdaff, when night overtook him on a lonely mountain road.

He knocked at one door after another asking for a night's lodging, while he jingled the halfpence in his pocket, but was everywhere refused.

Where was the boasted hospitality of Innishowen, which he had never before known to fail? It was of no use to be able to pay when the people seemed so churlish. Thus thinking, he made his way towards a light a little further on, and knocked at another cabin door.

An old man and woman were

seated one at each side of the fire.

'Will you be pleased to give me a night's lodging, sir?' asked Pat respectfully.

'Can you tell a story?' returned the old man.

'No, then, sir, I canna say I'm good at story-telling,' replied the puzzled tinker.

'Then you maun just gang further, for none but them that can tell a story will get in here.'

This reply was made in so decided a tone that Pat did not attempt to repeat his appeal, but turned away reluctantly to resume his weary journey.

'A story, indeed,' muttered he. 'Auld wives fables to please the weans!'

As he took up his bundle of tinkering implements, he observed a barn standing rather behind the dwelling-house, and, aided by the rising moon, he made his way towards it.

It was a clean, roomy barn, with a piled-up heap of straw in one corner. Here was a shelter not to be despised; so Pat crept under the straw, and was soon asleep.

He could not have slept very long when he was awakened by the tramp of feet, and, peeping cautiously through a crevice in his straw covering, he saw four immensely tall men enter the barn, dragging a body, which they threw roughly upon the floor.

They next lighted a fire in the middle of the barn, and fastened the corpse by the feet with a great rope to a beam in the roof. One of them then began to turn it slowly before the fire. 'Come on,' said he, addressing a gigantic fellow, the tallest of the four – 'I'm tired; you be to tak' your turn.'

'Faix an' troth, I'll no turn him,' replied the big man. 'There's Pat Diver in under the straw, why wouldn't he tak' his turn?'

With hideous clamour the four men called the wretched Pat, who, seeing there was no escape, thought

(*Above*) Andrew Coffey who suffers the practical jokes of a Far Darrig in *Celtic Fairy Tales.*
(*Left*) A group of little practical jokers beset an Irish milkmaid in Keightley's *Fairy Mythology.* (*Right*) Ill-luck will strike those who refuse a Far Darrig warmth by their fire – an illustration by John Pearson for *Whispers From Fairyland* (1877).

it was his wisest plan to come forth as he was bidden.

'Now, Pat,' said they, 'you'll turn the corpse, but if you let him burn you'll be tied up there and roasted in his place.'

Pat's hair stood on end, and the cold perspiration poured from his forehead, but there was nothing for it but to perform his dreadful task.

Seeing him fairly embarked in it, the tall men went away.

Soon, however, the flames rose so high as to singe the rope, and the corpse fell with a great thud upon the fire, scattering the ashes and embers, and extracting a howl of anguish from the miserable cook, who rushed to the door, and ran for his life.

He ran on until he was ready to drop with fatigue, when, seeing a drain overgrown with tall, rank grass, he thought he would creep in there and lie hidden till morning.

But he was not many minutes in the drain before he heard the heavy tramping again, and the four men came up with their burthen, which they laid down on the edge of the drain.

'I'm tired,' said one, to the giant; 'it's your turn to carry him a piece now.'

'Faix and troth, I'll no carry him,' replied he, 'but there's Pat Diver in the drain, why wouldn't he come out and tak' his turn?'

'Come out, Pat, come out,' roared all the men, and Pat, almost dead with fright, crept out.

He staggered on under the weight of the corpse until he reached Kiltown Abbey, a ruin festooned with ivy, where the brown owl hooted all night long, and the forgotten dead slept around the walls under dense, matted tangles of brambles and ben-weed.

No one ever buried there now, but Pat's tall companions turned into the wild graveyard, and began digging a grave.

Pat, seeing them thus engaged, thought he might once more try to escape, and climbed up into a hawthorn tree in the fence, hoping to be hidden in the boughs.

'I'm tired,' said the man who was digging the grave; 'here, take the spade', addressing the big man, 'it's your turn.'

'Faix an' troth, it's no my turn,' replied he, as before. 'There's Pat Diver in the tree, why wouldn't he come down and tak' his turn?'

Pat came down to take the spade, but just then the cocks in the little farmyards and cabins round the abbey began to crow, and the men looked at one another.

'We must go,' said they, 'and well is it for you, Pat Diver, that the cocks crowed, for if they had not, you'd just ha' been bundled into that grave with the corpse.'

Two months passed, and Pat had wandered far and wide over the county Donegal, when he chanced to arrive at Raphoe during a fair.

Among the crowd that filled the Diamond he came suddenly on the big man.

'How are you, Pat Diver?' said he, bending down to look into the tinker's face.

'You've the advantage of me, sir, for I havna' the pleasure of knowing you,' faltered Pat.

'Do you not know me, Pat?' Whisper – 'When you go back to Innishowen, you'll have a story to tell!'

The Haunted Realm

Ireland is one of the richest storehouses for ghost-lore in the world and it comes as no surprise to find that such a background should also have given us the greatest of all ghost story writers, Joseph Sheridan Le Fanu. From one end of the land to the other, from ruined castle to tiny thatched cottage, from crowded city thoroughfare to remote valley, the realm is filled with stories of ghosts, phantoms, spectres, wraiths and all manner of such spirits.

The Irish ghost is known as a *Thevshi* or *Tash* and can appear in human or animal form: indeed the country is particularly noted for the number of legends about phantom dogs, cats, horses (headless and otherwise), birds, rabbits and even insects such as butterflies! Quite a large percentage of these ghosts are said to be the spirits of people who died violent deaths, either having been murdered or committed suicide, and the Irish believe such souls are condemned to bring attention to themselves and their folly by haunting the place where they died as a lesson to others. In many country districts it is still held to be unwise to mourn for anyone for too long 'or else they will be kept from their rest and return as a ghost'. Hence, no doubt, the Irish delight in lively funeral parties!

It was from this great tradition that Joseph Sheridan Le Fanu (1814–73) drew the material for his series of supernatural novels and short stories which are still widely in print today. Le Fanu, who was born in Dublin, formed a deep interest and affection for country people during his youth, and from them learned many folk-tales which form the basis of stories like the eerie *The House by the Churchyard* (1863), the sinister *Uncle Silas* (1864) and the marvellous ghost story collections such as *In A Glass Darkly* (1872). Le Fanu was evidently most fascinated by the legends associated with Lough Gur in County Limerick, said to be as haunted a spot as any in Ireland. Even today it is not hard to appreciate why the air of mystery continues to surround this beautiful lake with castles, dolmens and stone circles on its banks. It can have changed little from Le Fanu's time and indeed the story which he relates here' 'The Magician Earl' concerning the Earl of Desmond who rises from his submerged castle at the bottom of the lake to haunt the vicinity, is still often repeated . . .

GHOSTS

(*Facing page*) An old print of ghosts around an Irish castle. (*Below, left*) An eighteenth-century print of a traveller in Galway accosted by an apparition. (*Below*) One of George Cruikshank's fine sketches of a ghost.

The Magician Earl

 T is well known that the great Earl of Desmond, though history pretends to dispose of him differently, lives to this hour enchanted in his castle, with all his household, at the bottom of the lake.

There was not, in his day, in all the world, so accomplished a magician as he. His fairest castle stood upon an island in the lake, and to this he brought his young and beautiful bride, whom he loved but too well; for she prevailed upon his folly to risk all to gratify her imperious caprice.

They had not been long in this beautiful castle, when she one day presented herself in the chamber in which her husband studied his forbidden art, and there implored him to exhibit before her some of the wonders of his evil science. He resisted long; but her entreaties, tears, and wheedlings were at length too much for him and he consented.

But before beginning those astonishing transformations with which he was about to amaze her, he explained to her the awful conditions and dangers of the experiment.

Alone in this vast apartment, the walls of which were lapped, far below, by the lake whose dark waters lay waiting to swallow them, she must witness a certain series of frightful phenomena, which once commenced, he could neither abridge nor mitigate; and if throughout their ghastly succession she spoke one word, or uttered one exclamation, the castle and all that it contained would in one instant subside to the bottom of the lake, there to remain, under the servitude of a strong spell, for ages.

The dauntless curiosity of the lady having prevailed, and the oaken door of the study being locked and barred, the fatal experiments commenced.

Muttering a spell, as he stood before her, feathers sprouted thickly over him, his face became contracted and hooked, a cadaverous smell filled the air, and, with heavy winnowing wings, a gigantic vulture rose in his stead, and swept round and round the room, as if on the point of pouncing upon her.

The lady commanded herself through this trial, and instantly another began.

The bird alighted near the door, and in less than a minute changed,

48

she saw not how, into a horribly deformed and dwarfish hag: who, with yellow skin hanging about her face and enormous eyes, swung herself on crutches towards the lady, her mouth foaming with fury, and her grimaces and contortions becoming more and more hideous every moment, till she rolled with a yell on the floor, in a horrible convulsion, at the lady's feet, and then changed into a huge serpent, with crest erect, and quivering tongue. Suddenly, as it seemed on the point of darting at her, she saw her husband in its stead, standing pale before her, and, with his finger on his lip, enforcing the continued necessity of silence. He then placed himself at his length on the floor, and began to stretch himself out and out, longer and longer, until his head nearly reached to one end of the vast room, and his feet to the other.

This horror overcame her. The ill-starred lady uttered a wild scream, whereupon the castle and all that was within it, sank in a moment to the bottom of the lake.

But, once in every seven years, by night, the Earl of Desmond and his retinue emerge, and cross the lake, in shadowy cavalcade. His white horse is shod with silver. On that one night, the earl may ride till daybreak, and it behoves him to make good use of his time; for, until the silver shoes of his steed be worn through, the spell that holds him and his beneath the lake, will retain its power.

When I was a child, there was still living a man named Teigue O'Neill, who had a strange story to tell.

He was a smith, and his forge stood on the brow of the hill, overlooking the lake, on a lonely part of the road to Cahir Conlish. One bright moonlight night, he was working very late, and quite alone. The clink of his hammer, and the wavering glow reflected through the open door on the bushes at the other side of the narrow road, were the only tokens that told of life and vigil for miles around.

In one of the pauses of his work, he heard the ring of many hoofs ascending the steep road that passed his forge, and, standing in his doorway, he was just in time to see a gentleman, on a white horse, who was dressed in a fashion the like of which

the smith had never seen before. This man was accompanied and followed by a mounted retinue, as strangely dressed as he.

They seemed, by the clang and clatter that announced their approach, to be riding up the hill at a hard hurry-scurry gallop; but the pace abated as they drew near, and the rider of the white horse who, from his grave and lordly air, he assumed to be a man of rank, and accustomed to command, drew bridle

(*Facing page: top*) Old print of the Earl of Desmond working black magic. (*Below*) Outstanding illustration by J. A. Pasquier for Le Fanu's story 'The Haunted Baronet' published in *Belgravia* (1870). (*Below*) Another picture from the *Belgravia* by E. Wagner for Le Fanu's ghost story 'Mr. Justice Harbottle' (1872).

and came to a halt before the smith's door.

He did not speak, and all his train were silent, but he beckoned to the smith, and pointed down to one of his horse's hoofs.

Teigue stooped and raised it, and held it just long enough to see that it was shod with a silver shoe; which, in one place, he said, was worn as thin as a shilling. Instantaneously, his situation was made apparent to him by this sign, and he recoiled with a terrified prayer. The lordly rider, with a look of pain and fury, struck at him suddenly, with something that whistled in the air like a whip; and an icy streak seemed to

Two of the superb illustration by W. V. Cockburn which illustrated Bram Stoker's now exceedingly rare collection of tales, *Under The Sunset* (1882). These were based on Irish legends, and show the development of his storytelling talent which was to culminate in *Dracula* in 1897.

traverse his body as if he had been cut through with a leaf of steel. But he was without scathe or scar, as he afterwards found. At the same moment he saw the whole cavalcade break into a gallop and disappear down the hill, with a momentary hurtling in the air, like the flight of a volley of cannon shot.

Here had been the earl himself. He had tried one of his accustomed stratagems to lead the smith to speak to him. For it is well known that either for the purpose of abridging or of mitigating his period of enchantment, he seeks to lead people to accost him. But what, in the event of his succeeding, would befall the person whom he had thus ensnared, no one knows.

Illustrations from books by two of Ireland's most famous ghost hunters. (*Below*) A picture for 'An Abbot's Ghost-Stories' from *Shane Leslie's Ghost Book* (1955). (*Right*) The tall, wizened ghost who terrified inhabitants of an Irish home as described by Elliott O'Donnell in his *Twenty Years' Experience as a Ghost Hunter* (1917).

'The Hag of the Mill' a marvellous
illustration by Arthur Rackham for
Irish Fairy Tales by James Stephens
(1920).

The Great Heroes of Old

The focal point for all the Irish legends about giants is, naturally enough, that amazing promontory known as the Giant's Causeway in County Antrim. Rightly considered as one of the great natural wonders of the world, the Causeway actually consists of closely packed greyish-coloured basalt columns which resulted from the crystallising of molten lava thrown up by a volcanic eruption during the Tertiary period of history. In all there are something like 40,000 hexagonal and pentagonal columns which are all interjointed and stretch almost half a mile out to sea.

Irish legend, however, has no time for such a prosaic explanation for the formation of the promontory, claiming it was built by the great Finn M'Coul (or Fann Mac Cuil as his name is perhaps more correctly spelt) as a bridge between Ireland and Scotland for the use of himself and the other Celtic giants. Much of the air of mystery about the Giant's Causeway has been retained over the years by the strange names given to certain of its formations – like the Giant's Organ, the Wishing Chair and the Coffin – and the fact that interaction of wind and sea can fill the place with weird and unearthly sounds.

As to the Irish giants themselves, old traditions say they developed from the ancient pagan heroes. W. B. Yeats explains this in *Irish Fairy and Folk Tales*: 'When the pagan gods of Ireland – the *Tuatha de Dannan* – robbed of worship and offerings, grew smaller and smaller in the popular imagination, until they turned into fairies, the pagan heroes grew bigger and bigger, until they turned into the giants.' The feats of these men are recounted in many of the Ossianic Legends – as they became known – and perhaps the most fascinating of these, featuring both Finn M'Coul and the Giant's Causeway, is the following tale included by Patrick Kennedy in his *Legendary Fictions of the Irish Celts* (1866).

(*Facing page*) John D. Batten illustration for the story of the giant Conall Yellowclaw in *Celtic Fairy Tales*. (*Below*) Finn M'Coul drawn by Arthur Rackham for the tale of 'The Little Brawl at Allen' in Stephens' *Irish Fairy Tales*.

GIANTS

Fann Mac Cuil and the Scotch Giant

HE great Irish *joiant*, Fann Mac Cuil, lived to be a middle-aged man, without ever meeting his match, and so he was as proud as a paycock. He had a great fort in the Bog of Allen, and there himself and his warriors would be playing soord and pot-lid, or shootin' bow-arras, or pitchin' big stones twenty or thirty miles off, to make a quay for the harbour of Dublin. One day he was quite down in the mouth, for his men were scattered here and there, and he had no one to wrestle or hurl, or go hunt along with him. So he was walking about very lonesome, when he sees a foot-messenger he had, coming hot-foot across the bog. 'What's in the *win*' (wind)?' says he. 'It's the great Scotch giant, *Far Rua*, that's in it,' says the other. 'He's coming over the big stepping stones that lead from Ireland to Scotland,* and you will have him here in less than no time. He heard of the great Fann Mac Cuil, and he wants to see which is the best man.' 'Oh, ho!' says Fann, 'I hear that the Far Rua is three foot taller nor me, and I'm three foot taller nor the tallest man in Ireland. I must speak to Grainne about it.'

Well, it wasn't long till the terrible Scotch fellow was getting along the stony road that led across the bog, with a sword as big as three scythe blades, and a spear the *lenth* of the house. 'Is the great Irish giant at home?' says he. 'He is not,' says Fann's messenger: 'he is huntin' stags at Killarney; but the vanithee is within, and will be glad to see you. Follow me, if you please.' In the hall they see a long *deal* (fir) tree, with an iron head on it, and a round block of wood, with an iron rim, as big as four cart wheels. 'Them is the shield and spear of Fann,' says the messenger. 'Ubbabow!' says the giant to himself.

* The Giant's Causeway, of which there are now visible only some slices at the two extremities. Those trustworthy chroniclers, the ancient bards, affirm that it is the work of the ancient Irish and Scotch men of might, laid down to facilitate their mutual visits.

Finn M'Coul building the Giants' Causeway – two illustrations by H. R. Heaton for *Irish Wonders* by D. R. McAnally.

'You're welcome, Far Rua,' says Grainne, as mild as the moon. 'Sit down, and take such fare as God sends.' So she put before him a great big griddle cake, with the griddle itself inside, that had a round piece cut out at one part of the rim; and for a beefsteak, she gave him a piece of a red deal plank, with a *skrimshin* of hard meat outside. The first bite the giant give at the cake, he broke three of his teeth; and when he tried the beef the other ones stuck so fast in the deal, he could not draw them out. 'By me soord, ma'am,' says he, 'this is hard diet you give your company.' 'Oh, Lord love you!' says she, 'the children here think nothing of it. Let us see if the infant would object.' So she takes the cake over where Fann was lying in the cradle, and offers him the part where the piece was taken out of the griddle. Well, he bit off the bread with the greatest ease, chawed it, and swallyed it, and smacked his lips after it, and then he winked one eye at Far Rua, 'Be the laws!' says the Scotchman to himself, 'these is wonderful people.'

Well, they didn't *stent* him in the drink any way. The jug of beer they laid before him would hold four gallons, and he emptied it out of spite at one offer, as he didn't get fair play at the bread and mate. 'I think,' says he, after his drink. 'I'd like to see how Fann and his men amuses themselves after dinner.' 'You must see that,' says the messenger. 'Step

out into the bawn, if it is agreeable to you.' Well, when they wor outside, the messenger pointed to four or five stones, the size and shape of a gate post. 'Them is their finger stones, that they do be casting to see who'll throw them farthest. It is a good throw when one of them reaches Dublin. But Fann does *moo-roon* (more than enough) sometimes; and you'll see some of them sticking up out o' the say where they light after a great fling. Maybe you'd like to try your hand.' He did try his hand, and after winding it round and round his head he let fly, and it went half a mile whistling through the air, and broke in a hundred smithereens on a big stone in the bog. 'You'll do well,' says the boy, 'when you come to your full growth, and get a year's practice or so with Fann.' 'To the d—— I pitch Fann and his finger stones!' says the big Red Man to himself.

'Well, is there any other way they divart themselves?' says the stranger. 'Oh, yes,' says the boy. 'Fann and his men does be throwing that handball (the ball was a round stone

Finn defeating his enemies – a picture by W. Small for *Legendary Fictions of the Irish Celts* by Patrick Kennedy (1886). (*Below*) The great Irish giant disguised as a child to fool the Scottish giant – a picture by John D. Batten for the story reprinted on these pages.

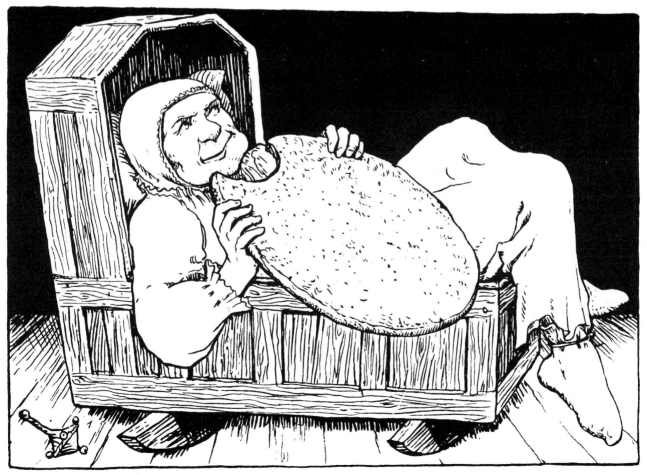

(*Above*) The one-eyed Irish giant, Sharvan, drawn by S. W. Fazain for *Irish Fairy Tales* by Edmund Leamy (1906).

(*Facing page, top*) John D. Batten illustration for the story of 'The Leeching of Kayn's Leg' from *More Celtic Fairy Tales*. (*Below*) 'Zaphir slays the Giant' a picture by W. V. Cockburn for Bram Stoker's *Under The Sunset* (1882).

that 'ud fill this hearth up to the mantel beam) from the bawn here over the house, and running round and catching it before it comes to the ground. Every miss counts one lost.' 'Wonderful quare people is the Irish,' said the big man. 'Maybe if it wouldn't go over with me at the first offer, it might break down the roof, and that 'ud annoy the vanithee. I'll pitch it up in the air here, and you can mark.' So he gave a heave. 'How high is it gone?' 'Up to the window sill.' 'Now?' 'Up to the eaves.' 'Dickens take it! Now where is it?' 'Oh, sir, it is on your head.' And indeed so it was, and levelled him also, and only he had a reasonable hard noggin of his own, it would be cracked in two with the souse the big stone gave it again' the ground.

He got up, and rubbed his poor skull, and looked very cross. 'I suppose Fann won't be home to-night.' 'Sir, he's not expected for a week.' 'Well, give the vanithee my compliments, and tell her I must go back without bidding her good bye, for fear the tide would overtake me crossing the Causeway.'

(*Above*) The Gruagach as seen by
John D. Batten in *Celtic Fairy Tales*.
(*Right*) The tiny version of the
Gruagach illustrated by W. H. Browne
in Keightley's *Fairy Mythology*.

The Creatures of Magic

The *Gruagach*, or *grogach* as it is known in Northern Ireland, is a creature with some of the attributes of the Scottish brownie or the English elf and has the ability to appear in the form of either a tiny being or 'a tall wizard champion' to quote one old legend.

In Ulster, for instance, the *grogach* is said to be about the size of a child, has a large head and a very soft body. Indeed, according to Lewis Spence in *The Fairy Tradition in Britain* (1948) 'he appears to have no bones at all when he comes tumbling down the hills'. He makes himself useful to mankind by carrying out domestic chores and is particularly good at threshing corn and herding cattle. The little creature apparently appreciates gifts of new clothes, presumably because he wears his own out with all the hard work!

Elsewhere in the country the word *Gruagach* is translated to mean a wizard, or man of magic, who can change his shape at will. A number of old Irish Hero Tales feature him as a dashing figure, dressed in regal clothes, who delights in performing extraordinary feats of magic and setting his protagonists seemingly impossible tasks.

An American folklorist, Jeremiah Curtin, was particularly interested in stories of the *Gruagach*, and collected a number for his books, including the following tale of the intrepid hero Micky Mor who encounters one in the form of a wizard. The story appeared in Curtin's *Hero Tales of Ireland* (1894).

THE GRUAGACH

The Amadan Mor and the Gruagach

T happened one day that while Micky Mor was out for a walk with his wife, Eilin Og, the sky grew so dark that it seemed like night, and he knew not where to go. But he went on till he came at last to a roomy dark glen. When he was inside in the glen, the greatest drowsiness that ever came over a man came over him.

'Eilin Og,' said he, 'come quickly under my head, for sleep is coming on me.'

'It is not sleep that is troubling you, but something in this great gloomy glen, where you were never before in your life.'

'Oh, Eilin Og, come quickly under my head.'

She came under his head, and he got a short nap of sleep. When he woke, hunger and thirst came on him greater than ever came upon any man ever born. Then a vessel came to him filled with food, and one with drink.

'Taste not the drink, take not a bite of the food, in this dark glen, till

you know what kind of a place is it.'

'Eilin Og, I must take one drink. I'll drink it whomsoever it vexes.'

He took a draught hard and strong from the vessel; and that moment the two legs dropped off Micky Mor from the knees down.

When Eilin Og saw this, she fell to wailing and weeping.

'Hold, hold, Eilin Og! silence your grief; a head or a leg will not be in the country unless I get my two legs again.'

The fog now dispersed, and the sky became clear. When he saw the sky clear, he knew where to go and he put his knife and spear and wife on the point of his shoulder. Then his strength and activity were greater, and he was swifter on his two knee than nine times nine other men that had the use of their whole legs.

While he was going on, he saw huntsmen coming towards him. A deer passed him. He threw the spear that he had in his hand; it went through the deer, in one side and out through the other. A white dog rushed straight after the deer. Micky Mor caught the deer and the dog, and kept them.

Now a young Gruagach, light and loose, was the first of the huntsmen to follow the white dog. 'Micky Mor,' said he, 'give me the white dog and the deer.'

'I will not,' said Micky. 'For it is myself that did the slaughter, strong and fierce, that threw the spear out of my right hand and put it through the two sides of the deer; and whoever it be, you or I, who has the strongest hand, let him have the white dog and the deer.'

'Micky Mor,' said Eilin Og, 'yield up the white dog and the deer.'

'I will,' said he, 'and more if you ask; for had I obeyed you in the glen, the two legs from the knees down would not have gone from me.'

The hunter, who was the Gruagach of Dun an Oir, was so glad to get his white dog and deer that he said, 'Come with me, Micky Mor, to my castle to dinner.'

The three were then passing along by the strand of Ard na Conye to the Gruagach's castle, when whom should they meet but a champion who began to talk with the men; but, seeing Eilin Og, he stopped on a sudden and asked Micky Mor, 'Who

(*Facing page*) Maurice Day's illustration for 'The Amadan Moir and the Gruagach' from *Hero Tales of Ireland* by Jeremiah Curtain (1921). (*Above*) 'The Unburied Legs', an illustration for a Munster legend included in *Tales of Fairy Land.*

is this woman with you? I think there is not another of such beauty in all the great world.'

'That is my wife, Eilin Og,' said Micky Mor.

'It is to find her that I am here, and to take her in spite of herself or her father,' said the champion.

'If you take her, you will take her in spite of me,' said Micky Mor; 'but what champion are you with such words?'

'I am Maragach of the Green Gloves from Great Island. I have travelled the world twice, and have met no man to match me. No weapons have hurt my skin yet or my body. Where are your arms of defence in this great world, Micky Mor?'

'I have never wished for a weapon but my own two fists that were born with me.'

'I name you now and forever,' said Maragach, 'the Big Fool (Amadan Mor).'

'No talk of the mouth performs deeds of valour, but active, strong bones. Let us draw back now, and close with each other. We shall know then who is the best man; and if there is valour in you, as you say, you dirty little Maragach, I will give you a blow with strength that will open your mouth to the bone.'

They went towards each other then threateningly, and closed like two striking Balors or two wild boars in the days of the Fenians, or two hawks of Cold Cliff, or two otters of Blue Pool. They met in close, mighty struggle, with more screeching than comes from a thousand. They made high places low, and low places high. The clods that were shot away by them, as they wrestled, struck out the eye of the hag in the Eastern World, and she spinning thread at her wheel.

Now Maragach drew his sword strong, keen-edged, and flawless; this sword always took with the second blow what it did not cut with the first; but there was no blow of it that time which the Big Fool did not dodge, and when the sun was yellow at setting, the sword was in small bits, save what remained in the hand

of the champion. That moment the Fool struck the champion a blow 'twixt neck and skull, and took the head off his body.

The three went on then to the castle of Dun an Oir (Castle of Gold), and had a fine dinner. During the dinner they were discoursing and telling tales; and the Gruagach's wife took greatly to heart the looks that her husband was giving Eilin Og, and asked, 'Which is it that you will have, Negil Og's daughter or the wife of the Big Fool?'

Said Eilin Og to the Gruagach's wife, 'This man's name is not the Big Fool in truth or in justice, for he is a hero strong and active; he is master of all alive and of every place. All the world is under his command, and I with the rest.'

'If he is all this, why did he let the legs go from him?' asked the Gruagach's wife.

Eilin Og answered, 'I have said that he has high virtues and powers; and only for the drink that was brought him in the dark lonely glen, he would not have let the legs go from him.'

The Gruagach was in dread that the Big Fool might grow angry over their talks, and that enchantment would not get the upper hand of strength, and said, 'Give no heed to woman's talk, Micky Mor, but guard my castle, my property, and my wife, while I go to the Dun of the Hunt and return.'

'If any man comes in in spite of me,' said Micky Mor, 'while you are absent, believe me, he will not go out in spite of me till you return.'

The Gruagach went off then, and with the power of his enchantment put a heavy sleep on Micky Mor.

'Eilin Og,' said he, 'come quickly under my head, for over-strong sleep has come on me.'

Eilin Og came under his head, and he got a short nap of sleep. The Gruagach returned soon in a different form altogether, and he took a kiss from his own wife.

'Oh,' said Eilin Og to her husband, 'you are in your sleep, and it is to my grief that you are in it, and not at the right time.'

Micky Mor heard her, and he, between sleeping and waking, gave one leap from his body when he heard Eilin Og's words, and stopped at the door. It would have been a greater task to break any anvil or block made by blacksmith or woodworker, than to force the Big Fool from the door.

'Micky Mor,' said the Gruagach, disguised, 'let me out.'

'I will not let you out till the Gruagach of Dun an Oir comes home, and then you will pay for the kiss that you took from his wife.'

'I will give you a leg swift and strong as your own was; it is a leg I took from the Knight of the Cross when he was entering his ship.'

'If you give me one of my legs swift and strong as ever, perhaps I may let you go out.'

That moment the Fool got the leg. He jumped up then, and said, 'This is my own leg, as strong and as active as ever.'

'The other leg now, or your head!' said Micky Mor.

The Gruagach gave him the other leg, blew it under him with power of enchantment. Micky Mor jumped up. 'These are my own legs in strength and activity. You'll not go out of this now till the Gruagach comes, and you pay for the kiss you took from his wife.'

'I have no wish to knock a trial out of you,' said the Gruagach, and he changed himself into his own form again. 'You see who I am; and I am the huntsman who took your legs with the drink that you got from the cup, and now we are equal.'

(*Below and facing page*) Two interpretations of Irish Little People – by George Cruikshank and the American artist, Virgil Finlay.

Melmoth the Doomed Wanderer

The story of the Wandering Jew who, according to legend, insulted Christ on his way to Calvary, and was condemned to wander about the world until His second coming, is known in most nations – and the Irish, like many others, have reports of this lonely figure being seen in their country. But what Ireland has specifically contributed to this strange story is undoubtedly the finest of all fantasy novels about an immortal man, *Melmouth the Wanderer*, written by a Dublin clergyman, Charles Robert Maturin, in 1820.

This marvellous three-volume work about a man doomed to eternal youth was supposedly based on a sighting of the Wandering Jew in Dublin which came to the attention of Charles Maturin. Though weighed down with financial problems and the demanding duties of being curate at St Peter's Church in the city, Maturin (1782–1824) poured all his writing skills, his vivid imagination and his knowledge of folklore into the story. Its impact at the time of publication and continuing influence to this day has done much to sustain public interest in the mysterious figure of the Wandering Jew.

Melmoth the Wanderer is primarily the story of a rich, dissipated Irishman who signs a pact with the Devil in return for eternal youth. But as the years pass by, so his friends change, the conditions of life alter – but there is no change whatsoever in himself. His initial delight at being immortal then slowly turns to an all-consuming horror as he begins to realise the implications of living forever. Thus he sets out on a journey around the world to find death – a journey which takes him through a variety of horrors from pagan rites in India to the terrors of the Spanish Inquisition – until finally he finds peace in a most unexpected manner. The extract from Maturin's book which follows gives a clear idea of its originality and atmosphere of mounting horror.

(*Facing page*) A modern portait of Melmoth the Wanderer (1966) and (*left*) a traditional portrait of the Wandering Jew by Edward Zier (1885).

THE IMMORTAL MAN

The Wanderer's Dream

HE dreamed that he stood on the summit of a precipice, whose downward height no eye could have measured, but for the fearful waves of a fiery ocean that lashed, and blazed, and roared at its bottom, sending its burning spray far up, so as to drench the dreamer with its sulphurous rain. The whole glowing ocean below was alive – every billow bore an agonising soul, that rose like a wreck or a putrid corpse on the waves of earth's oceans – uttered a shriek as it burst against that adamantine precipice – sunk – and rose again to repeat the tremendous experiment! Every billow of fire was thus instinct with immortal and agonising existence – each was freighted with a soul, that rose on the burning wave in torturing hope, burst on the rock in de-

spair, added its eternal shriek to the roar of that fiery ocean, and sunk to rise again – in vain, and – for ever!

Suddenly the Wanderer felt himself flung halfway down the precipice. He stood, in his dream, tottering on a crag midway down the precipice – he looked upward, but the upper air (for there was no heaven) showed only blackness unshadowed and impenetrable – but, blacker than that blackness, he could distinguish a gigantic outstretched arm, that held him as in sport on the ridge of that infernal precipice, while another, that seemed in its motions to hold fearful and invisible conjunction with the arm that grasped him, as if both belonged to some being too vast and horrible even for the imagery of a dream to shape, pointed upwards to a dial-plate fixed on the top of that precipice, and which the flashes of that ocean of fire made fearfully conspicuous. He saw the mysterious single hand revolve – he saw it reach the appointed

period of 150 years – (for on this mystic plate centuries were marked, not hours) – he shriked in his dream, and, with that strong impulse often felt in sleep, burst from the arm that held him to arrest the motion of the hand.

In the effort he fell, and falling grasped at aught that might save him. His fall seemed perpendicular – there was nought to save him – the rock was as smooth as ice – the ocean of fire broke at its foot! Suddenly a group of figures appeared, ascending as he fell. He grasped at them successively; – first Stanton – then Walberg – Elinor, Mortimer – Isidora – Monçada – all passed him – to each he seemed in his slumber to cling in order to break his fall – all ascended the precipice. He caught at each in his downward flight, but all forsook him and ascended.

His last despairing reverted glance was fixed on the clock of eternity – the upraised black arm seemed to push forward the hand – it arrived at its period – he fell – he sunk – he blazed – he shrieked! The burning

(*Facing page*) Another of Edward Zier's pictures of the Wandering Jew legend, and below a climactic moment from Melmoth the Wanderer. (*Above*) 'The Wandering Jew in Ireland' by Andre Castaigne (1904).

waves boomed over his sinking head, and the clock of eternity rung out its awful chime – 'Room for the soul of the Wanderer!' – and the waves of the burning ocean answered, as they lashed the adamantine rock – 'There is room for more!' – The Wanderer awoke.

The Leprechaun – a modern
impression by Bill Terry published in
Other Worlds, 1950.

The Marvellous Shoe~Maker

The word *Leprechaun* is now widely and erroneously used to describe all the different kinds of Irish fairies. In fact, as is shown in the pages of this book, he is just one specific member of the fairy family, and it is most probable that his name derived from the words *leith bhrogan*, the one-shoemaker. (To be fair it has also been suggested that the word could have come from *Luacharma'n*, the Irish for pigmy.)

Such arguments aside, he is without doubt a fairy shoemaker and in most traditional stories he is seen at work on a single shoe. There is also a consensus of opinion that the *Leprechaun* is of low descent, his father being an evil spirit and his mother a degenerate fairy. Writing in *Irish Wonders* (1888), D. R. McAnally describes the little creature thus: 'He is of diminutive size, about three feet high, and is dressed in a little red jacket or roundabout, with red breeches buckled at the knee, grey or black stockings, and a hat, cocked in the style of a century ago, over a little, old, withered face. Round his neck is an Elizabethan ruff, and frills of lace are at his wrists. On the wild west coast, where the Atlantic winds bring almost constant rains, he dispenses with ruff and frills and wears a frieze overcoat over his pretty red suit, so that unless on the look-out for the cocked hat, "ye might pass a *Leprechaun* on the road and never know it's himself that's in it at all".' Sometimes, it is said, his activities are mischievous and tricky and he always thwarts any human beings who try to capture him. Apart from such pranks as riding on dogs, sheep and goats, and causing small accidents in the house, he can, if he chooses, be most helpful to those families who believe in him. By way of contrast he has a well-known dislike of all teachers who deny his existence!

In different parts of Ireland he sometimes goes under slightly varied names such as the *Logheryman* in the northern counties, the *Lurigadawne* in Tipperary, and the *Luricawne* in Kerry. But his general characteristics seem to be much the same throughout the nation as W. B. Yeats has noted, 'The *Leprechaun* makes shoes continually and has grown very rich. Many treasure-crocks, buried of old in war-time, has he now for his own. In the early part of this century, according to T. Crofton Croker, in a newspaper office in Tipperary, they used to show a little shoe forgotten by a *Leprechaun*.' The story selected next, 'The Field of Boliauns' from Joseph Jacob's *Celtic Fairy Tales* (1892) is typical of the many hundreds of such tales which exist, and recounts yet another encounter between man and *Leprechaun* – with the inevitable result.

LEPRECHAUNS

(*Left*) The traditional idea of the Leprechaun as depicted in the German translation of Crofton Croker's book, *Fairy Legends*, prepared by the Brothers Grimm and published as *Irische Elfenmärchen*.

'The Wee Piper' a whimsical
illustration by the talented John D.
Batten for *Celtic Fairy Tales*.

The Field of Boliauns

NE fine day in harvest – it was indeed Lady-day in harvest, that everybody knows to be one of the greatest holidays in the year – Tom Fitzpatrick was taking a ramble through the ground, and went along the sunny side of a hedge; when all of a sudden he heard a clacking sort of noise a little before him in the hedge. 'Dear me,' said Tom, 'but isn't it surprising to hear the stonechatters singing so late in the season?' So Tom stole on, going on the tops of his toes to try if he could get a sight of what was making the noise, to see if he was right in his guess. The noise stopped; but as Tom looked sharply through the bushes, what should he see in a nook of the hedge but a brown pitcher, that might hold about a gallon and a half of liquor; and by-and-by a little wee teeny tiny bit of an old man, with a little *motty* of a cocked hat stuck upon the top of his head, a deeshy daushy leather apron hanging before him, pulled out a little wooden stool, and stood up upon it, and dipped a little piggin into the pitcher, and took out the full of it, and put it beside the stool, and then sat down under the pitcher, and began to work at putting a heel-piece on a bit of a brogue just fit for himself. 'Well, by the powers,' said Tom to himself, 'I often heard tell of the Leprecauns, and, to tell God's truth, I never rightly believed in them – but here's one of them in real earnest. If I go knowingly to work, I'm a made man. They say a body must never take their eyes off them, or they'll escape.'

Tom now stole on a little further, with his eye fixed on the little man just as a cat does with a mouse. So when he got up quite close to him, 'God bless your work, neighbour,' said Tom.

The little man raised up his head, and 'Thank you kindly,' said he.

'I wonder you'd be working on the holiday!' said Tom.

'That's my own business, not yours,' was the reply.

'Well, may be you'd be civil enough to tell us what you've got in

the pitcher there?' said Tom.

'That I will, with pleasure,' said he; 'it's good beer.'

'Beer!' said Tom. 'Thunder and fire! where did you get it?'

'Where did I get it, is it? Why, I made it. And what do you think I made it of?'

'Devil a one of me knows,' said Tom; 'but of malt, I suppose, what else?'

'There you're out. I made it of heath.'

'Of heath!' said Tom, bursting out laughing; 'sure you don't think me to be such a fool as to believe that?'

'Do as you please,' said he, 'but what I tell you is the truth. Did you never hear tell of the Danes?.'

'Well, what about *them*?' said Tom.

'Why, all the about them there is, is that when they were here they taught us to make beer out of the heath, and the secret's in my family ever since.'

'Will you give a body a taste of your beer?' said Tom.

'I'll tell you what it is, young man, it would be fitter for you to be looking after your father's property than to be bothering decent quiet people with your foolish questions. There now, while you're idling away your time here, there's the cows have broke into the oats, and are knocking the corn all about.'

Tom was taken so by surprise with this that he was just on the very point of turning round when he re-collected himself; so, afraid that the like might happen again, he made a grab at the Lepracaun, and caught him up in his hand; but in his hurry he overset the pitcher, and spilt all the beer, so that he could not get a taste of it to tell what sort it was. He then swore that he would kill him if he did not show him where his money was. Tom looked so wicked and so bloody-minded that the little man was quite frightened; so says he, 'Come along with me a couple of fields off, and I'll show you a crock of gold.'

So they went, and Tom held the Lepracaun fast in his hand, and never took his eyes from off him, though they had to cross hedges and ditches, and a crooked bit of bog, till

Two illustrations by H. R. Heaton for D. R. McAnally's story in *Irish Wonders* of Tim O'Donovan of Kerry who captured a Leprechaun and was then outwitted by him when he searched for a pot of gold . . .

EUG. BURNAND

at last they came to a great field all full of boliauns, and the Lepracaun pointed to a big boliaun, and says he, 'Dig under that boliaun, and you'll get the great crock all full of guineas.'

Tom in his hurry had never thought of bringing a spade with him, so he made up his mind to run home and fetch one; and that he might know the place again he took off one of his red garters, and tied it round the boliaun.

Then he said to the Lepracaun, 'Swear ye'll not take that garter away from that boliaun.' And the Lepracaun swore right away not to touch it.

'I suppose,' said the Lepracaun, very civilly, 'you have no further occasion for me?'

'No,' says Tom; 'you may go away now, if you please, and God speed you, and may good luck attend you wherever you go.'

'Well, good-bye to you, Tom Fitzpatrick,' said the Lepracaun; 'and much good may it do you when you get it.'

So Tom ran for dear life, till he came home and got a spade, and then away with him, as hard as he could go, back to the field of boliauns; but when he got there, lo and behold! not a boliaun in the field but had a red garter, the very model of

his own, tied about it; and as to digging up the whole field, that was all nonsense, for there were more than forty good Irish acres in it. So Tom came home again with his spade on his shoulder, a little cooler than he went, and many's the hearty curse he gave the Lepracaun every time he thought of the neat turn he had served him.

74

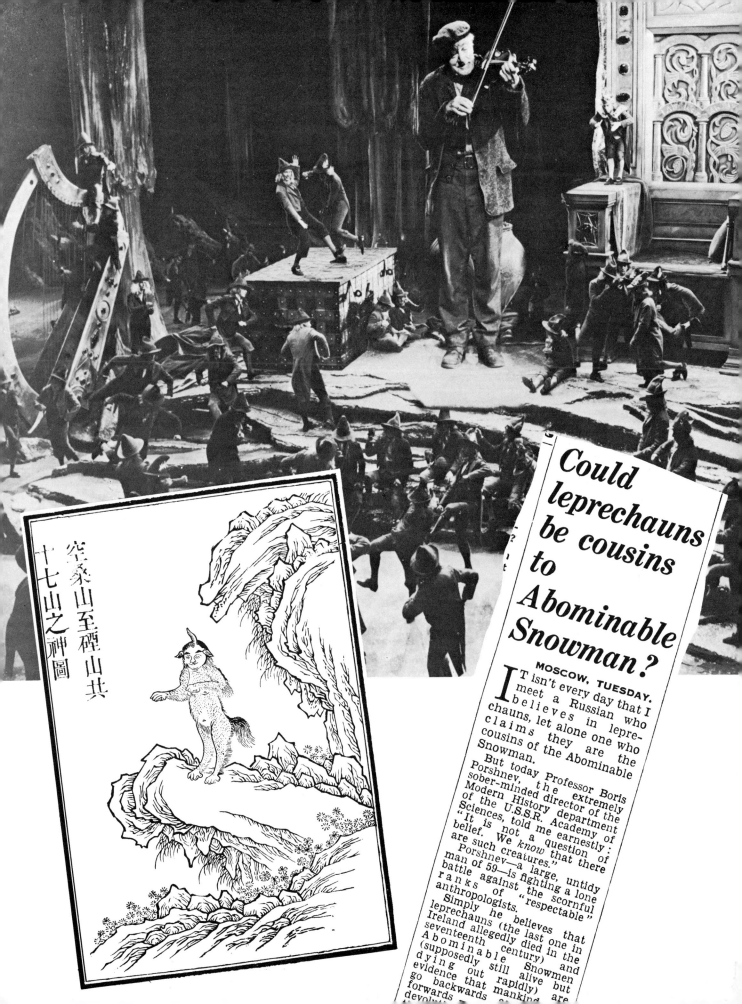

空桑山至砠山共
十七山之神圖

Could leprechauns be cousins to Abominable Snowman?

MOSCOW, TUESDAY.

IT isn't every day that I meet a Russian who believes in leprechauns, let alone one who claims they are the cousins of the Abominable Snowman.

But today Professor Boris Porshnev, the extremely sober-minded director of the Modern History department of the U.S.S.R. Academy of Sciences, told me earnestly: "It is not a question of belief. We *know* that there are such creatures."

Porshnev—a large, untidy man of 59—is fighting a lone battle against the scornful ranks of "respectable" anthropologists.

Simply he believes that leprechauns (the last one in Ireland allegedly died in the seventeenth century) and Abominable Snowmen (supposedly still alive but dying out rapidly) are evidence that mankind go backwards as well as forwards
devolu

The Sea Maiden

The Beautiful Maidens of the Sea

There are few more fabled creatures in folklore than mermaids, and Ireland, where they are called merrows or occasionally *Suire*, sea maidens, has a long and fascinating history concerning them. The word merrow, or *Moruadh* as it is written in Irish, comes from *muir*, the sea, and *oigh*, meaning a maid.

According to tradition mermaids are always beautiful, the only features in any way affecting this attraction being their tales, olive-tinted skin and webbed fingers. Mermen, the *Murdhuach*, on the other hand, have fine torsos but the most ugly features: pig's eyes, red noses, green teeth and seaweed coloured hair. Perhaps not surprisingly it is said that mermaids prefer seamen or coastal dwellers for their lovers, and there are a number of Irish families who are claimed to be descended from such unions – including the O'Flaherty and O'Sullivan families of Kerry and the Macnamaras from Clare.

W. B. Yeats in his *Irish Fairy and Folk Tales* notes that 'Near Bantry, in the last century, there is said to have been a woman covered all over with scales like a fish, who was descended from such a marriage. Sometimes the mermaids come out of the sea, and wander about the shore in the shape of little hornless cows. They have, when in their own shape, a red cap, called a *cohullen druith*, usually covered with feathers. If this is stolen, they cannot again go down under the waves.'

Ireland's most famous story of a merrow concerns the mermaid caught in Belfast Lough in AD 588. Apparently she had been seen in the area for a number of years and so often heard singing beneath the waters, that she proved an irresistable attraction to a group of men who rowed out into the water and caught her in a net. Much to their surprise, they learned she had originally been a little human girl called Liban whose family had died in a flood, but she had survived beneath the waves and gradually been transformed into a mermaid. The men christened the girl Murgen and put her on display in a tank for all to see. A number of miracles were later attributed to her and after death she was re-named 'St Murgen'.

The following unusual story of a mermaid who is still believed to appear on an island in the Shannon is recounted by Lady Wilde in her *Ancient Legends of Ireland* (1888).

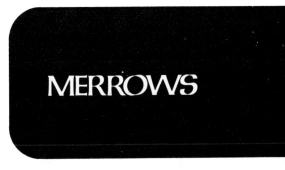

MERROWS

(*Facing page*) John D. Batten's illustration of 'The Sea Maiden'. (*Above*) A delightful mermaid from *Legends and Superstitions of the Sea and Sailors* by Fletcher S. Bassett (1885). (*Left*) An unusual engraving of a Mermaid and a Merman from *Curious Creatures* (1812).

The Dead Soldier

HERE is an island in the Shannon, and if a mermaid is seen sitting on the rocks in the sunshine, the people know that a crime has been committed somewhere near; for she never appears but to announce ill-luck, and she has a spite against mortals, and rejoices at their misfortunes.

One day a young fisherman was drawn by the current towards the island, and he came on a long streak of red blood, and had to sail his boat through it till he reached the rocks where the mermaid was seated; and then the boat went round and round as in a whirlpool, and sank down at last under the waves.

Still he did not lose consciousness. He looked round and saw that he was in a beautiful country, with tall plants growing all over it; and the mermaid came and sang sweetly to him, and offered him wine to drink, but he would not taste it, for it was red like blood. Then he looked down, and to his horror he saw a soldier lying on the floor with his throat cut; and all round him was a pool of blood, and he remembered no more till he found himself again in his boat drifting against a hurricane, and suddenly he was dashed upon a rock, where his friends who were in search of him found him, and carried him home. There he heard a strange thing: a soldier, a deserter from the Athlone Barracks, being pursued had cut his throat and flung himself over the bridge into the river; and this was the very man the young fisher had seen lying a corpse in the mermaid's cave. After this he had no peace or comfort till he went to the priest, who exorcised him and gave him absolution; and then the wicked siren of the rocks troubled him no more, though she still haunts the islands of the Shannon and tries to lure victims to their death.

(*Top*) Mermaids at play – a W. H. Brooke illustration from *Fairy Mythology* and (*below*) a mermaid tries to lure an unsuspecting human into the sea: from *Legends and Superstitions of the Sea and Sailors*

A beautiful mermaid offers her child to a fisherman – an illustration by Rachel Duff from *The Celtic Dragon Myth* by D. F. Campbell (1911).

What Came of Picking Jessamine

Water Beasts & Wurrums

According to the local historian, Dr P. W. Joyce, 'legends of acquatic monsters are very ancient among the Irish people' and he has pointed out that several places in the country actually got their names because of the belief in such creatures. Lough Derg, the Red Lake, in Donegal, for instance, commemorates the slaughter of a monster by the great Finn M'Coul which left the waters red with its blood.

Irish water monsters are generally known as *Peisthas* and they vary in size from a few feet to fifty yards and more, while in appearance they look like anything from a snake, a crocodile to a gigantic sea horse! One of the most famous of them is described by W. R. Le Fanu in his book, *Seventy Years of Irish Life* (1893): 'That dreadful beast, the Wurrum — half-fish, half-dragon — still survives in many a mountain lake — seldom seen, indeed, but often heard. Near our fishing quarters in Kerry there are two such lakes, one the beautiful little lake at the head of the Blackwater River, called Lough Brin, or Bran as he is now called, the dreadful wurrum which inhabits it.' The monster's name apparently derived from an old story that Finn's hunting dog Bran was drowned in this self-same lake, and there are stories of local people seeing the creature right up to the present day. (Finn, of course, made almost a profession of slaying serpents and monsters throughout Ireland as the stories of his adventures relate.)

Over the years, such interest has been generated in Irish water beasts that a number of lakes have been subjected to scientific study and examination to try and prove the existence of the creatures which local traditions say live in them. Among these are Lough Mask, Lough Ree, Lough Bray, Lough Graney and several stretches of water in the province of Connaught.

The following interesting story of a *peistha* is recounted by 'Lageniensis' (Canon John O'Hanlon) in his *Irish Local Legends* (1896).

MONSTERS

(*Facing page*) A water beast strikes! A superb illustration by H. J. Ford (1900). (*Left*) John D. Batten picture for the story of 'The Sea Maiden' in *Celtic Fairy Tales*. (*Over page*) An encounter with a 'Devil Fish' from *Whispers From Fairyland* (1877).

The Peistha Discomforted

ARDLY any deep lake in Ireland is without the occupancy of an uncouth monster, seldom seen on the surface, but often observed in motion, far down in the depths of the water. Imagination is frequently exercised by the peasantry, to divine its exact form, which is supposed to differ in species from that of any known denizen of the deep; and mystery shrouding its functions, the *Peistha* is dreaded as a malignant demon, always bent upon mischief, and especially towards the human race. The boatmen cast many a furtive glance downwards, to see that it approach not within stroke of their oars, as they greatly desire to give it a wide berth. Any provoked hostility on their part is apt to procure a dangerous retaliation; and in his frequented waters, the *Peistha* is believed to be master of the situation.

At one time St Molua, who travelled much through Ireland on his mission of founding churches, visited the ancient Drumsneachta, now Drumsna, in the County of Monaghan. In a neighbouring lake, he saw two boys swimming. But, advancing on them, and with a forefront large as a boat of considerable size, appeared the monster of that lake, as if about to devour them. Not wishing to terrify the boys, he shouted to them: 'Swim, my boys, with all speed towards me, so that I may reward the one who shall first arrive, and that I may know who will swim the fastest.' Both struck out towards him, and soon gained the shore. No sooner had they landed, than Molua reached them his hand. Having landed safely, they looked back towards the lake, and were greatly frightened at seeing the monster, which had almost gained upon them. Immediately the saint raising his staff struck the *Peistha* with it on the breast, and it gave a terrific roar. Filled with excitement and alarm, one of the boys died on the instant. However, the holy man prayed for him, and afterwards he came to life. But, a malison he pronounced on the monster ordering it to return and to remain under the waters of that lake. Thenceforward it was condemned never to molest man or beast to the Day of Judgment.

(*Below*) Finn M'Coul battles with a many-headed monster during one of his many adventures. A John D. Batten illustration from *Celtic Fairy Tales*.

(*Above*) The monarch named
Conn who fought the monsters of
Lough Erne – a picture by James
Torrance for 'The Story of Conn-Eda'
by Abraham McCoy (1893). Another
lake monster by John D. Batten for
'Fair, Brown and Trembling' from
Celtic Fairy Tales.

The Nightmare Steed

The Phouka, or *Puca*, is essentially an animal spirit, and is mostly seen in the form of a horse, though he can appear as a goat, an ass, a bull, and even an eagle or bat! The name is believed to derive from the word *poc*, a he-goat, and it has been suggested that he was the forefather of Shakespeare's 'Puck'. He lives on isolated mountains or among old ruins, and there are a number of places in Ireland known as 'Poula Phouka' or the Hole of the Phouka. The best known of these spots is a waterfall of this name formed by the Liffey in County Wicklow.

The spirit's main purpose seems to be to carry unsuspecting victims for wild rides on his back, having crept up behind them and tossed them on to his back. Country people often still warn their children that they should not pick and eat blackberries after Michaelmas Day (September 29) as the decay which begins to affect them at this time has been caused by the Phouka.

In some parts of Ireland the spirit is said to be more mischievous than dangerous, and in the main helpful and well-disposed towards humanity – as long as he is treated with respect, of course. As historian Douglas Hyde (1860–1949) has written in *Beside the Fireside* (1920), 'In an old story we read that "out of a certain hill in Leinster, there used to emerge as far as his middle, a plump, sleek, terrible steed, and speak in human voice to each person about November-day, and he was accustomed to give intelligent and proper answers to such as consulted him concerning all that would befall them until the November of the next year. And the people used to leave gifts and presents at the hill until the coming of Patrick and the holy clergy". This tradition appears to be a cognate one with that of the Puca.'

One of the best stories of a Phouka is the one which follows and is found in the old Irish volume, *Leabhar Sgeulaigheachta*, here translated by Douglas Hyde.

THE PHOUKA

(*Facing page*) The King Bryan Boru who tamed a Phouka – an illustration by H. R. Heaton for *Irish Wonders* by D. R. McAnally. (*Left*) Another Heaton illustration for the same story, entitled 'Taming The Pooka'. (*Above*) The Phouka seen in the form of a bull, a picture by Rowel Friers for *Ulster Folklore* (1951).

The Piper and the Puca

N the old times, there was a half fool living in Dunmore, in the county Galway, and although he was excessively fond of music, he was unable to learn more than one tune, and that was the 'Black Rogue'. He used to get a good deal of money from the gentlemen, for they used to get sport out of him. One night the piper was coming home from a house where there had been a dance, and he half drunk. When he came to a little bridge that was up by his mother's house, he squeezed the pipes on, and began playing the 'Black Rogue' (*an rógaire dubh*). The Púca came behind him, and flung him up on his own back. There were long horns on the Púca, and the piper got a good grip of them, and then he said –

'Destruction on you, you nasty beast, let me home. I have a ten-penny piece in my pocket for my mother, and she wants snuff.'

'Never mind your mother,' said the Púca, 'but keep your hold. If you fall, you will break your neck and your pipes.' Then the Púca said to him, 'Play up for me the "Shan Van Vocht" (*an t-seann-bhean bhocht*).'

'I don't know it,' said the piper.

'Never mind whether you do or you don't,' said the Púca. 'Play up, and I'll make you know.'

The piper put wind in his bag, and he played such music as made himself wonder.

'Upon my word, you're a fine music-master,' says the piper then; 'but tell me where you're for bringing me.'

'There's a great feast in the house of the Banshee, on the top of Croagh Patric to-night,' says the Púca, 'and I'm for bringing you there to play music, and, take my word, you'll get the price of your trouble.'

'By my word, you'll save me a journey, then,' says the piper, 'for Father William put a journey to Croagh Patric on me, because I stole the white gander from him last Martinmas.'

The Púca rushed him across hills and bogs and rough places, till he brought him to the top of Croagh Patric. Then the Púca struck three blows with his foot, and a great door opened, and they passed in together, into a fine room.

The piper saw a golden table in the middle of the room, and hundreds of old women (cailleacha) sitting round about it. The old women rose up, and said, 'A hundred thousand welcomes to you, you Púca of November (na Samhna). Who is this you have with you?'

'The best piper in Ireland,' says the Púca.

One of the old women struck a blow on the ground, and a door opened in the side of the wall, and what should the piper see coming out but the white gander which he had stolen from Father William.

'By my conscience, then,' says the piper, 'myself and my mother ate every taste of that gander, only one wing, and I gave that to Moy-rua (Red Mary), and it's she told the priest I stole his gander.'

The gander cleaned the table, and carried it away, and the Púca said, 'Play up music for these ladies.'

The piper played up, and the old women began dancing, and they were dancing till they were tired. Then the Púca said to pay the piper, and every old woman drew out a gold piece, and gave it to him.

'By the tooth of Patric,' said he, 'I'm as rich as the son of a lord.'

'Come with me,' says the Púca, 'and I'll bring you home.'

They went out then, and just as he was going to ride on the Púca, the gander came up to him, and gave him a new set of pipes. The Púca was not long until he brought him to Dunmore, and he threw the piper off at the little bridge, and then he told him to go home, and says to him, 'You have two things now that you never had before – you have sense and music (*ciall agus ceól*).'

The piper went home, and he knocked at his mother's door, saying, 'Let me in, I'm as rich as a lord, and I'm the best piper in Ireland.'

'You're drunk,' said the mother.

'No, indeed,' says the piper, 'I haven't drunk a drop.'

The mother let him in, and he gave her the gold pieces, and, 'Wait now,' says he, 'till you hear the music I'll play.'

He buckled on the pipes, but instead of music, there came a sound as if all the geese and ganders in Ireland were screeching together. He wakened the neighbours, and they were all mocking him, until he put on the old pipes, and then he played melodious music for them; and after that he told them all he had gone through that night.

The next morning, when his mother went to look at the gold pieces, there was nothing there but the leaves of a plant.

The piper went to the priest, and told him his story, but the priest would not believe a word from him, until he put the pipes on him, and then the screeching of the ganders and geese began.

'Leave my sight, you thief,' says the priest.

But nothing would do the piper till he would put the old pipes on him to show the priest that his story was true.

He buckled on the old pipes, and he played melodious music, and from that day till the day of his death, there was never a piper in the county Galway was as good as he was.

The beautiful *Leanhaun Shee*, a
painting by Ernest Wallcousins.

The Spell of the Fairy Mistress

In Ireland, fairies tend to be divided into two categories: Solitary and Trooping Fairies. The former are generally malignant or ominous creatures who keep to themselves and are invariably dressed in red – the best known examples being the *Cluricaune*, the *Far Darrig* and the *Leprechaun*. The latter congregate in groups, dress in green, can be of varying sizes, and are mostly friendly disposed towards human beings. They are also said to love Hurling matches!

But apart from the three types of Solitary Fairies mentioned above, there are two other important kinds to be found in the country. The first is the *Fear Gorta*, or Man of Hunger. He is described as a very emaciated figure who appears during periods of national disaster or hardship, and famine times in particular. He wanders from town to town, begging alms or small gifts of food, and it is said that anyone who makes him a gift will ensure good luck for themselves.

A more attractive fairy by far is the *Leanhaun Shee*, or Fairy Mistress. Indeed it is her very beauty that is dangerous, for her purpose is to make mortal men fall in love with her. Such is her loveliness, it is said, that her charms are very hard to resist, but once a man is trapped in her embrace, the *Leanhaun Shee* gradually draws the life from him and he wastes away. The only way to escape this inexorable process is for the victim to find another man to take his place. As W. B. Yeats has written, 'She is the Gaelic muse, for she gives inspiration to those she persecutes. The Gaelic poets die young, for she is restless, and will not let them remain long on earth – this malignant phantom.'

The legend of the *Leanhaun Shee* is explained next by Lady Wilde from *Ancient Legends of Ireland* (1888).

SOLITARY FAIRIES

(*Facing page*) The charming and seductive Leanhaun Shee as drawn by Linley Sambourne for *Friends and Foes From Fairyland* (1886). A modern version of this little enchantress by Hannes Bok for *Other Worlds*, 1950.

Eodain the Poetess

 HE *Leanan-Sidhe*, or the spirit of life, was supposed to be the inspirer of the poet and singer, as the *Ban-Sidhe* was the spirit of death, the foreteller of doom.

The *Leanan-Sidhe* sometimes took the form of a woman, who gave men valour and strength in the battle by her songs. Such was Eodain the poetess, by whom Eugene, king of Munster, gained complete victory over his foes. But afterwards he gave himself up to luxury and pleasure, and went away to Spain, where he remained nine years, and took to wife the daughter of the king of Spain. At the end of that time he returned to Ireland with a band of Spanish followers. But he found his kingdom plundered and ruined, and the revellers and drunkards were feasting in his banquet hall, and wasting his revenues for their pleasures while the people starved. And the whole nation despised the king, and would not hear his words when he sat down in his golden chair to give just judgment for iniquity. Then Eugene the king, in his deep sorrow and humiliation, sent for Eodain the poetess to come and give him counsel. So Eodain came to him, and upheld him with her strong spirit, for she had the power within her of the poet and the prophet, and she said –

'Arise now, O king, and govern like a true hero, and bring confusion

on the evil workers. Be strong and fear not, for by strength and justice kings should rule.'

And Eugene the king was guided by her counsel and was successful. And he overthrew his enemies and brought back peace and order to the land. For the strength of the *Leanan-Sidhe* was in the words of Eodain, the power of the spirit of life which is given to the poet and the prophet, by which they inspire and guide the hearts of men.

The Irish Trooping Fairies are said to be particularly fond of the game of Hurling as these amusing sketches by John D. Batten show. They appeared in *More Celtic Fairy Tales*. (*Facing page*) A grimly evocative engraving of the terrible *Fear Gorta*, 'The Man of Hunger', as drawn by H. K. Browne ('Phiz') for *Irish Legends*.

(*Above*) The traditional idea of the Irish phantom island as drawn by W. H. Brooke for Keightley's *Fairy Mythology*. (*Right*) *Tir-Nan-Og*, 'The Country of Youth' illustrated in Crofton Croker's *Fairy Legends*. (*Top*) Illustration by H. R. Heaton for D. R. McAnally's story 'The Enchanted Island' reprinted overleaf.

The Phantom Islands

There are several stories in Irish legend of Phantom Islands located somewhere off the coast in the Atlantic Ocean which are said to be the homes of fairies and supernatural beings of all kinds.

The most famous of these is known as *Breasail*, once the original home of the Fomorians and the Firbolgs. It is believed to lie off the south-west of Ireland and only appears above the waves from time to time. St Brendan, that intrepid Irish saint and seaman, who is reputed to have sailed to America before Columbus, was apparently one of the people who visited the island. He described it as an earthly paradise which was caused to sink by an outbreak of sinning among its inhabitants! Since then it only reappears to warn of impending disaster. Not far from *Breasail* is *Flath-Innis*, the Noble Isle, which was once the abode of Druids who unfortunately caused it to sink when they uttered certain terrible incantations thereby upsetting its balance!

Phantom lands are also supposed to exist beneath the waters of a number of Irish lakes, and these places are known in local folklore as *Tir-Nan-Og*. 'The Country of Youth', where supernatural beings live unaffected by the passage of time. Accounts tell of the bard Oisin who visited one of these places and dwelt there for three hundred years. Immediately he returned to dry land, however, he was instantly doubled up with extreme age and barely had time to record his adventures before he died. Since his visit, many other people have claimed to have seen the submerged 'Country of Youth' or heard the sound of its bells ringing up from the waters of various lakes. Old traditions have it that such enchanted places are to be found in the green depths of Lough Neagh, Lough Corrib, Lough Gur and the Lake of Killarney.

Probably the most informative of all the pieces about these mysterious places is 'The Enchanted Island' by D. R. McAnally from his *Irish Wonders* (1888).

TIR-NAN-OG

The Enchanted Island

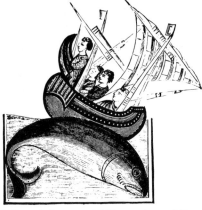

(*Above*) A very old illustration of St. Brendan, the Irish Saint who is said to have found America before Columbus, and visited a number of phantom islands on the voyage. This island proved to be a whale!

N the afternoon of Sunday, July 7, 1878, the inhabitants of Ballycotton, County Cork, were greatly excited by the sudden appearance, far out at sea, of an island where none was known to exist. The men of the town and island of Ballycotton were fishermen and knew the sea as well as they knew the land. The day before, they had been out in their boats and sailed over the spot where the strange island now appeared, and were certain that the locality was the best fishing-ground they had.

'And still they gazed, and still the wonder grew,' for the day was clear and the island could be seen as plainly as they saw the hills to the north. It was rugged, in some parts rocky, in others densely wooded; here and there were deep shadows in its sides indicating glens heavily covered with undergrowth and grasses. At one end it rose almost precipitously from the sea; at the other, the declivity was gradual; the thick forest of the mountainous portion gave way to smaller trees, these to shrubs; these to green meadows that finally melted into the sea and became indistinguishable from the waves.

Under sail and oar, a hundred boats put off from the shore to investigate; when, as they neared the spot, the strange island became dim in outline, less vivid in colour, and at last vanished entirely, leaving the wonder-stricken villagers to return, fully convinced that for the first time in their lives they had really seen the Enchanted Island. For once there was a topic of conversation that would outlast the day, and as the story of the Enchanted Island passed from lip to lip, both story and island grew in size till the latter was little less than a continent, containing cities and castles, palaces and cathedrals, towers and steeples, stupendous mountain ranges, fertile valleys, and wide spreading plains; while the former was limited only by the patience of the listener, and embraced the personal experience, conclusions, reflections, and observations of every man, woman, and child in the parish who had been fortunate enough to see the island, hear of it, or tell where it had been seen elsewhere.

For the Enchanted Island of the west coast is not one of those ordinary, humdrum islands that rise out of the sea in a night, and then, having come, settle down to business on scientific principles, and devote their attention to the collection of soil for the use of plants and animals. It disdains any such commonplace course as other islands are content to follow, but is peripatetic, or, more properly, seafaring, in its habits, and as fond of travelling as a

The warrior O'Donoghue who found a phantom land in the Lake of Killarney. A picture by James Torrance for 'The Legend of O'Donoghue' by T. Crofton Croker.

sailor. As its own sweet will it comes, and, having shown itself long enough to convince everybody who is not an 'innocent entirely' of its reality, it goes without leave-taking or ceremony, and always before boats can approach near enough to make a careful inspection. This is the invariable history of its appearance. No one has ever been able to come close to its shores, much less land upon them, but it has been so often seen on the west coast, that a doubt of its existence, if expressed in the company of coast fishermen, will at once establish for the sceptic a reputation for ignorance of the common affairs of every-day life.

In Cork, for instance, it has been seen by hundreds of people off Ballydonegan Bay, while many more can testify to its appearance off the Bay of Courtmacsherry. In Kerry, all the population of Ballyheige saw it a few years ago, lying in Tralee Bay, between Kerry Head and Brandon's Head, and shortly before, the villagers of Lisneakeabree, just across the bay from Ballyheige, saw it between their shore and Kerry Head, while the fishermen in Saint Finan's Bay and in Ballinskelligs are confident it has been seen, if not by themselves, at least by some of their friends. It has appeared at the mouth of the Shannon, and off Carrigaholt in Clare, where the people saw a city on it. This is not so remarkable as it seems, for, in justice to the Enchanted Island, it should be stated that its resemblance to portions of the neighbouring land is sometimes very close, and shows that the 'enchanter' who has it under a spell knows his business, and being determined to keep his island for himself changes its appearance as well as its location in order that his property may not be recognised nor appropriated.

In Galway, the Enchanted Island has appeared in the mouth of Ballinaleame Bay, a local landlord at the time making a devout wish that it would stay there. The fishermen of Ballynaskill, in the Joyce Country, saw it about fifteen years ago, since when it appeared to the Innisshark islanders. The County Mayo had seen it, not only from the Achille Island cliffs, but also from Downpatrick Head; and in Sligo, the fishermen of Ballysadare Bay

know all about it, while half the population of Inishcrone still remember its appearance about twenty years ago. The Inishboffin islanders in Donegal say it looked like their own island, 'sure two twins couldn't be liker', and the people on Gweebarra Bay, when it appeared there, observed along the shore of the island a village like Maas, the one in which they lived. It has also appeared off Rathlin's Island, on the Antrim coast, but, so far as could be learned, it went no further to the east, confining its migrations to the west coast between Cork on the south and Antrim on the north.

Concerning the island itself, legendary authorities differ on many material points. Some hold it to be 'a rale island sure enough', and that its exploits are due to 'jommethry or some other inchantmint', while op-

ponents of this materialistic view are inclined to the opinion that the island is not what it seems to be, that is to say, not 'airth an' shtones, like as thim we see, but only a deludh erin' show that avil sper'ts, or the divil belike, makes fur to desave us poor dishsolute craythers'. Public opinion on the west coast is therefore strongly divided on the subject, unity of sentiment existing on two points only; that the island has been seen, and that there is something quite out of the ordinary in its appearance. 'For ye see, yer Anner,' observed a Kerry fisherman, 'it's agin nacher fur a rale island to be comin' and goin' like a light in a bog, an' whin ye do see it, ye can see through it, an' by jagers, if it's a thrue island, a mighty quare wan it is an' no mishtake.'

The Bard Oisen who visited 'The County of Youth'. A picture by Stephen Reid from *Myths and Legends of the Celtic Race* by T. W. Rolleston (1912).

An Irish vampire by John D. Batten
for *More Celtic Fairy Tales.*

The Terror of the Red Blood Sucker

The vampire tradition in Ireland goes back to the days of antiquity and there are stories about the *Dearg-due*, or 'Red Blood Sucker' as the creature is called, to be found in several counties. The people naturally went in great fear of them, and it was customary to pile stones upon the graves of those suspected of being vampires so they could not rise up and terrorise the living. In parts of Ireland it is still believed that the newly-buried dead can become active again at the New Year, leaving their coffins and going in search of human blood.

Ireland's most famous vampire is the beautiful female *Dearg-due* who is said to lie buried near to Strongbow's Tree in Waterford. Her tomb is in the graveyard of the little church nearby, and legend says she arises on certain nights of the year, using her fatal beauty to lure unsuspecting men into her arms where she sucks the lifeblood from their necks.

Two of the greatest vampire tales were actually written by Irishmen, *Carmilla* by Joseph Sheridan Le Fanu, the master of the ghost story, and *Dracula* by Bram Stoker (1847–1912). It is probable that both these Dublin men knew the local legends of the *Dearg-due*, and certainly Le Fanu's story written in 1872 deals specifically with the activities of a beautiful female vampire. Stoker's *Dracula* (published in 1897) is, of course, the classic vampire novel, and although set in Transylvania, is undoubtedly influenced by Irish stories that the author heard as a boy, and which he recounted in his now excessively rare first book of grim tales, *Under The Sunset* (1882).

One of the most fascinating of true Irish vampire stories appeared as recently as October 1925 in the magazine, *The Occult Review*. In it, the author R. S. Breene recounts the extraordinary tale of one of the very few vampires ever seen appearing before nightfall . . .

(*Above*) The *Dearg-Due*, or 'Red Blood-sucker', from a nineteenth century engraving.

(*Left*) The vampire about to strike in Le Fanu's famous story, 'Carmilla'. The illustration is by D. H. Friston for *The Dark Blue*, 1871–2.

(*Following page*) A striking engraving of the grim business of burying a vampire at a cross roads to prevent it from rising to prey on the living.

VAMPIRES

The Man from the Grave

A MEMBER of the family of M—, a farming connection, had been ordained to the priesthood, and eventually was put in charge of a little hill parish by the local Bishop. He is reputed to have been a quiet, inoffensive man, not given much to the companionship of his flock, and rather addicted to reading and study. His parishioners listened with edification to his sermons, brought their children to him for the rite of baptism, made their confession to him at intervals, and took the sacred bread of the Holy Communion from his hands on Sundays and the greater festivals of the Church . . . He was hospitable to strangers, and had frequently placed beds in his little parochial house at the disposal of belated travellers and even tramps. Yet no one in his immediate neighbourhood would have thought of going to see him socially. They went to him on the Church's business, or they did not go at all. He was, in a word, respected, though not greatly liked.

When he had little more than passed his fiftieth birthday he suddenly fell ill and died, after a brief confinement to his chamber. He was buried with all the simple pomp that surrounds the obsequies of an Irish country priest. His body, I should have said, was removed before the funeral to his mother's house, which was several miles distant from his parish. It was from there that the funeral took place. It was a sad picture when the body came home to the aged mother, whose chief pride in her later years had been her 'boy in the Church', the priest; and it was sadder still when the coffin set out once more from the whitewashed farmhouse, to carry its occupant upon his last journey to the rocky graveyard in the hills where all his kin had laid their bones for generations. According to custom, all the male and female members of the connection accompanied the corpse. The bereaved mother was left to her thoughts for the rest of the day in the house of death . . .

Meanwhile the funeral cortège wended its slow way (a long procession of traps, jaunting-cars and spring-carts) towards its destination in the mountains. They did not waste much time in getting their sad task over and done, but they had a

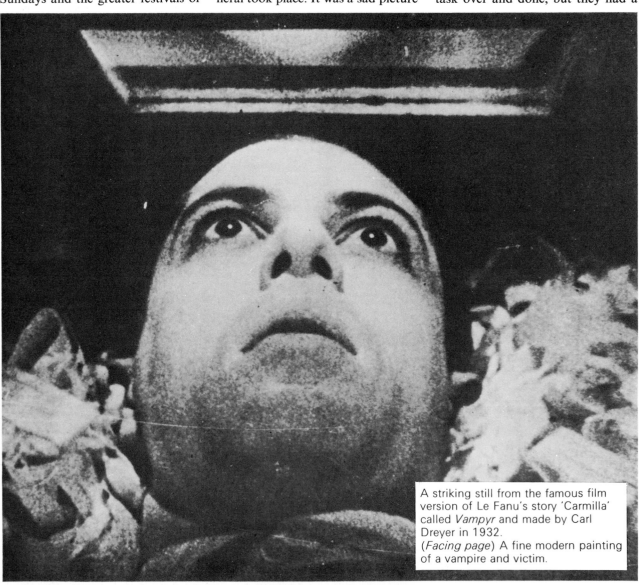

A striking still from the famous film version of Le Fanu's story 'Carmilla' called *Vampyr* and made by Carl Dreyer in 1932.
(*Facing page*) A fine modern painting of a vampire and victim.

EUBANKS

long road to traverse, and the sun was already declining in the heavens as they climbed the last succession of hills on the way to the homestead they had left in the morning ... They were all sober, but many of them, particularly the womenfolk, had fallen asleep. Night was already in the air. The shadows were lengthening below the hill-crests, but upon the white limestone highway everything was still in broad daylight. At the foot of a slope the mourners in the first cars suddenly became aware of a solitary figure coming down towards them walking rapidly. As the distance between them and the pedestrian lessened they were surprised to see that he was a priest. They knew of no priest who could be there at such a time. Those who had taken part in the ceremonies at the grave had not come so far with them on the return journey. They began to speculate as to who the man could be. Remarks were exchanged, and meanwhile the newcomer had met the foremost car. Two men were awake in it. There could be no mistake. *They saw at once, and quite clearly, that they were face to face with the man whom they had laid in his grave two or three hours before.* He passed them with his head slightly averted, but not sufficiently to prevent them from making absolutely certain of his identity, or from noting the intense,

livid pallor of his skin, the hard glitter of his wide-open eyes, *and* the extraordinary length of his strong, white teeth, from which the full red lips seemed to be writhed back till the gums showed themselves. He was wearing, not the grave-clothes in which he had been attired for his burial, but the decent black frock-coat and garments to match in which they had last seen him alive. He passed down the long line of vehicles, and finally disappeared round the turn in the road. Someone in every loaded trap or car had seen him; in short, most of those who had been awake and on that side. A thrill of terror passed through the whole party. With hushed voices and blanched cheeks they pushed on quickly, now only anxious to get under some sheltering roof and round some blazing hearth before dread night should fall upon them.

Their first call was at the M— farmhouse. In the front was a little porch built round the door, with a small narrow window on either side. About this they gathered, and hurriedly decided to say no word of what had happened to the bereaved mother. Then someone knocked, but received no answer. They knocked again, but still being denied admittance, they began to be uneasy. At last someone thought of peeping in through one of the little side-windows, when he saw old

Mrs M— lying face downward on the floor. They hesitated no longer, but literally broke in, and it was some little time before they were able to bring her round again to consciousness. This, briefly, is what she told them.

About half an hour earlier, she had heard footsteps on the flags outside, followed by a loud challenging knock. She was surprised that they should have returned so soon, and, besides, she had been expecting the sound of the cars approaching. She decided that it could not be any of the family, and so, before opening, she looked out at the side. There, to her horror, she saw her dead son standing in the broad daylight much as she had last seen him alive. He was not looking directly at her. But she, too, noted the extraordinary length of his teeth, the cold blaze of his eyes, I might say the wolfishness of his whole bearing, and the deathly pallor of his skin. Her first instinctive movement was to open the door. Then fear swept over her, swamping even her mother-love. She felt her limbs giving way under her, and quickly sank into the oblivion in which she lay until they found her.

(*Opposite*) Christopher Lee, the best known modern Dracula of the screen, photographed making 'Dracula, Prince of Darkness'. This is a painting of Bela Lugosi who also helped immortalise Dracula in a series of films in the 1930s.

The Lure of the Marsh Lights

The Water Sheerie is just one of several names given in Ireland to strange little phosphorescent creatures which are believed to be omens of death when they are seen by anyone. They mostly appear in the vicinity of churchyards or over marshy land, and sometimes take on the shape of dancing flames as they glide from cover to cover.

These lights are by no means peculiar to Ireland, and in other parts of Europe including Britain they are called 'Jack O'Lantern', 'Will-O'-the-Wisp', Corpse Candles and *Ignis Fatuus*, 'Foolish Fire'.

In parts of Ireland, the Water Sheerie is said to be a ghostly figure wearing a fiery garment and carrying a perpetually burning hank of straw in his hand. He is the soul of someone who has been refused admission to either heaven or hell, and condemned to wander the land luring those unwise enough to follow him. His other names include *teine sionniic*, fox fire; *teine side*, fairy fire; *Seán na gealaige*, Jack of the Bright Light; *Liam na lasóige*, William with the Little Flame, etc. He has been reported since the earliest times, is referred to by Shakespeare in *The Tempest*, and was known to the poet Milton who wrote that the creature:

> 'Misleads the amazed night wanderer from his way,
> To bogs and mires, and oft through pond and pool.'

The Water Sheerie got his evil reputation because he is said to lure travellers to disaster or death in swamp land by giving them the impression his glow is the light of a distant dwelling place. He has also been known to appear around buildings at night and this is said to signify a forthcoming death in the family. The only way he can be driven off is with an iron implement such as a knife or a cross.

Over the years, scientists have frequently tried to dismiss the Water Sheerie as being nothing more than burning marsh gas or another gas known as phosphuretted hydrogen. But against this explanation is the fact that these gases do not catch light of their own accord, and in any case no flame could dance from place to place as they are said to do . . .

Probably the most delightful account about these creatures is the tale related by Lord Dunsany concerning a conversation he had with an Irish storyteller called Paddy O'Hone and published in his book *The Man Who Ate The Phoenix* (1949). A later section in this book, 'Worlds of Wonder', is devoted to Dunsany, the master of fantasy.

WATER SHEERIE

(*Facing page*) An old Irish engraving of a Water Sheerie or Will O' The Wisp. (*Left*) Another of Arthur Rackham's fine illustrations for *Irish Fairy Tales*.

The Jack O'Lanterns

 ELL,' I said to Paddy O'Hone one day when we were talking, 'there was something I wanted to ask you about. It seems to me that Ireland is full of strange things that have never been properly classified, and that, as you can see them all, it might be a good thing to have some proper description made of them.'

'Ah,' said Paddy, 'I won't say I see as many as that. We all know there used to be a great number of queer things in all parts of the country; but this is not the same as the old days, and I only see what are still going around. Just an odd thing now and again. But I would be happy to describe any one of them that you were interested in.'

'Well,' I said, 'I heard that you met a leprechaun.'

'I did, sure,' said Paddy.

'And I was wondering,' I went on, 'if you saw any other queer things down by the bog; so that they could be properly classified.'

Paddy thought for a moment.

'I mind the time I saw jack-o'-lanterns,' he said. 'And more nor once I saw them.'

'What were they like?' I asked.

(*Top*) Another Will O' The Wisp trying to lure an unwary traveller to his doom. An illustration by T. H. Thomas for *British Goblins*. (*Right*) The cross provides a method of protection against the Water Sheerie.

(*Above*) A Water Sheerie luring man and horse into a bog – a picture by W. H. Brooke for *Fairy Mythology*. (*Right*) Disaster brought about by following a Will O' The Wisp – a nineteenth-century engraving.

'Ah, small brown things about the size of a hare, or maybe a bit larger, leaping over the bog with a lantern.'

'What I should like to hear,' I said, 'and what the public would really be interested in, if you would tell me something about it, is the home life of a jack-o'-lantern.'

'Home life, is it?' said Paddy O'Hone. 'Ah, sure, they mostly sleep by day.'

'But at night?' I asked.

'Ah,' said Paddy, 'sure, it's mostly guiding they're interested in, to judge from their talk; guiding men that are out late on the bog. They never talked of anything else, only how they had guided men.'

'And where do they guide them?' I asked.

'To their own homes, sure,' said Paddy. 'To the jack-o'-lanterns' homes, I mean.'

'And where are their homes?' I said.

'Among the red mosses and the green mosses,' said Paddy, 'that lie over the deep places. You can always tell their homes by the bright mosses. Sure, the mosses are just like thatches to jack-o'-lanterns; wherever you see a bit of scarlet moss, or a bit that's greener nor grass, there's a jack-o'-lantern living under it.'

'And they guide men there?' I asked, so as to get it quite clear.

'Sure, they talked of nothing else,' said Paddy.

'What did they talk like?' I asked.

'They talked very melodious and faint and strange,' he said; 'with a voice I couldn't describe to you, but if once you heard it you could never mistake it for any other sound in the world, unless for a snipe drumming.'

'Why do they guide men to the deep parts of the bog?' I asked. For I wanted to get some understanding of the life of a jack-o'-lantern, and it is difficult to understand much of any creature unless you know its principal motive.

'Sure, they are jealous of the holy angels and of all blessed things,' said Paddy. 'They don't want them to be getting the souls of men, and they want to keep them for themselves.'

'What good does that do them?'

And it was then that I think I got from Paddy O'Hone some glimpse of the home life of a jack-o'-lantern.

'Sure, they talk to them through the long evening of eternity,' said Paddy, 'in the deeps below the bright mosses. That's what they're doing when the bograil is croaking and night coming on in the world: the jack-o'-lanterns and the spirits of men they have guided talk there in the deeps for ever.'

'But what do they talk about?' I asked.

'Politics,' said Paddy O'Hone.

(*Top*) One of the many tricks the Water Sheerie can play – making little flames dance on a hay cart. (*Right*) Fairy Lights playing on the masts of an old sailing ship – an engraving from *Legends and Superstitions of the Sea and Sailors.* (*Facing page*) A delightful modern interpretation of the Will O' The Wisp by Cecily Peele from *Encyclopedia of British Bogies* (1978).

Man Beasts in Wolf-Land

Ancient records indicate that from the earliest times, Ireland had a very large population of wolves running wild, and one particular book, *The Travels of Cosmo* (1669), says the country was known far and wide as 'Wolf-Land'. For this reason the people reared a special breed of dog, a tall, rough greyhound of exceptional size and power, the Wolfhound, to hunt and kill the fierce packs. It is perhaps not surprising, therefore, that werewolves, men with the ability to change into animals, are recorded from antiquity down through the years of the country's history.

The metamorphosis of man into wolf, known as *Lycanthropy*, was supposed to take place at night when the moon was full, and in Ireland it was believed that it ran in families. In a thirteenth-century hexameter poem, 'Wonders of Ireland', it is stated, 'There are certain men of the Celtic race who have marvellous power which comes to them from their forebears. For by an evil craft they can at will change themselves into the shape of wolves with sharp tearing teeth, and often thus transformed will they fall upon poor defenseless sheep, but when folk armed with clubs and weapons run to attack them shouting lustily, then do they flee and scur away apace. Now when they are minded to transform themselves they leave their own bodies, straitly charging their friends neither to move or touch them at all, however lightly, for if this be done never will they be able to return to their human shape again. If whilst they are wolves anyone hurts or wounds them, then upon their own bodies the exact wound or mark can plainly be seen. And with much amaze have they been espied in human form with great gobbets of raw bleeding flesh champed in their jaws.'

Another old manuscript, the *Cóir Anmann*, speaks about *Laignech Fáelad*, men who could change into wolf-shapes, and who, along with their offspring, used to attack herds of cattle and sheep; while the English historian, William Camden, refers somewhat sceptically to stories of 'The Wolf Men of Tipperary'. Undoubtedly, though, the most famous Irish werewolf story is that related by Giraldus Cambrensis (c. 1147–1223) the historian and ecclesiastic. He accompanied Prince John on his tour of Ireland in 1185 and wrote a remarkable history of the country, its people and legends entitled *Topographia Hibernica*, in the course of which he recounts the following unusual and rather touching variation on the traditional werewolf tale.

WEREWOLVES

Two old engravings of the werewolf attacking a man and a woman. These 'Man Beasts' are known throughout Ireland. (*Following pages*) A superb illustration of another werewolf by H. J. Ford for Andrew Lang's *The Red Romance Book* (1935).

The Werewolves of Ossory

BOUT three years before the arrival of Prince John in Ireland, it chanced that a certain priest, who was journeying from Ulster towards Meath, was benighted in a wood that lies on the boundaries of Meath. While he, and the young lad his companion, were watching by a fire they had kindled under the leafy branches of a large tree, there came up to them a wolf who immediately addressed them in the following words: 'Do not alarm yourselves and do not be in any way afraid.' You need not fear, I say, where there is no reason for fear.' The travellers none the less were thrown in a great damp and were astonished. But the wolf reverently called upon the Name of God. The priest then adjured him, straitly charging him by Almighty God and in the might of the Most Holy Trinity that he should do them no sort of harm, but rather tell them what sort of creature he was who spake with a human voice.

The wolf replied with seemly speech, and said: 'In number we are two, to wit a man and a woman, natives of Ossory, and every seven years on account of the curse laid upon our folk by the blessed Abbot S. Natalis, a brace of us are compelled to throw off the human form and appear in the shape of wolves. At the end of seven years, if perchance these two survive they are able to return again to their homes, reassuming the bodies of men, and another two must needs take their place. Howbeit my wife, who labours with me under this sore visitation, lies not far from hence, grievously sick. Wherefore I beseech you of your good charity to comfort her with the aid of your priestly office.'

When he had so said, the wolf led the way to a tree at no great distance, and the priest followed him trembling at the strangeness of the thing. In the hollow of the tree he beheld a wolfen, and she was groaning piteously mingled with sad human sighs. Now when she saw the priest she thanked him very courteously and gave praise to God Who had vouchsafed her such consolation in her hour of utmost need.

The priest then shrived her and gave her all the last rites of Holy Church so far as the houselling. Most earnestly did she entreat him that she might receive her God, and that he would administer to her the crown of all, the Body of the Lord.

The priest, however, declared that he was not provided with the holy viaticum, when the man-wolf, who had withdrawn apart for a while, came forward and pointed to the wallet, containing a mass-book and some consecrated Hosts which, according to the use of his country, the good priest was carrying suspended from his neck under his clothing. The man-wolf entreated him not to deny them any longer the Gift of God, which it was not to be questioned, Divine Providence had sent to them. Moreover to remove all doubt, using his claw as a hand, he drew off the pelt from the head of the wolfen and folded it back even as far down as the navel, whereupon there was plainly to be seen the body of an old woman. Upon this the priest, since she so instantly besought him, urged though it may be more by fear than by reasoning, he-sitated no longer but gave her Holy Communion, which she received most devoutly from his hands. Immediately after this the man-wolf rolled back the skin again, fitting it to its former place.

These holy rites having been duly rather than regularly performed, the man-wolf joined their company by the fire they had kindled under the tree and showed himself a human being not a four-footed beast. In the early morning, at cock-light he led them safely out of the wood, and when he left them to pursue their journey he pointed out to them the best and shortest road, giving them directions for a long way. In taking leave also, he thanked the priest most gratefully and in good set phrase for the surpassing kindness he had shown, promising moreover that if it were God's will he should return home (and already two parts of the period during which he was under the malediction had passed) he would take occasion to give further proofs of his gratitude.

As they were parting the priest inquired of the man-wolf whether the enemy (the English invader) who had now landed on their shores would continue long to possess the land. The wolf replied: 'On account of the sins of our nation and their enormous wickedness the anger of God, falling upon an evil generation, hath delivered them into the hands of their enemies. Therefore so long as this foreign people shall walk in the way of the Lord and keep His commandments, they shall be safe and not to be subdued; but if – and easy is the downward path to iniquity and nature prone to evil – it come to pass that through dwelling among us they turn to our whoredoms, then assuredly will they provoke the wrath of the Lord upon themselves also.'

The Devil's Dark Legions

Witchcraft has been a part of the Irish supernatural since very early times, and all such folk have been said to be in league with the Devil and under his command. Throughout all this period, witches have been credited with the power to turn themselves into animals such as cats or hares so as to work their mischief unobserved. They are also said to be much practised in the art of weaving *pishogues*, or spells, and can communicate with evil spirits who will do their bidding.

In the light of the country's long witchcraft tradition, it is perhaps surprising that it suffered very little actual witch persecution, unlike the rest of the British Isles and much of Europe, during the terrible era which stretched from the end of the Middle Ages and through the sixteenth and seventeenth centuries when hundreds of thousands of men, women and children were hideously tortured and executed on the scantiest evidence that they might somehow have sold their souls to the Devil. The Evil One is, none the less, a potent figure in Irish history, and there are many localities with traditions of his appearance and intervention in the lives of mankind.

According to W. B. Yeats in *Irish Fairy and Folk Tales*, one of the most important if bizarre items in a witch's armoury is the 'Hand of Glory' of which he writes, 'The Spells of the witch smell of the grave. One of the most powerful is the charm of the dead hand. With a hand cut from a corpse they, muttering words of power, will stir a well and skim from its surface a neighbour's butter. A candle held between the fingers of the dead hand can never be blown out . . . this is useful to robbers.'

Ireland has also had its famous magicians and dabblers in the black arts like the Earl of Desmond whose ghost now haunts Lough Gur (see Joseph Sheridan Le Fanu's story in the section, 'The Haunted Realm') and indeed interest in mysticism and the occult has continued right up to the present time. Belief in witchcraft has similarly persisted, and nowhere has this been more tragically underlined than at the turn of the century in the case of the Clonmel Witch Burning when an unfortunate woman who was believed to be a witch was tortured and slowly roasted to death by her husband and some relatives.

From the rich storehouse of Irish witch stories comes our final tale by Patrick Kennedy from his collection, *Fictions of the Irish Celts* (1866).

WITCHES

(*Facing page*) A striking painting by W. Heath Robinson of a witch and her child. (*Right*) Illustration by H. R. Heaton for 'A Witches' Excursion' from D. R. McAnally's *Irish Wonders*.

The Witches' Excursion

HEMUS RUA (Red James) awakened from his sleep one night by noises in his kitchen. Stealing to the door, he saw half-a-dozen old women sitting round the fire, jesting and laughing, his old housekeeper, Madge, quite frisky and gay, helping her sister crones to cheering glasses of punch. He began to admire the impudence and imprudence of Madge, displayed in the invitation and the riot, but recollected on the instant her officiousness in urging him to take a comfortable posset, which she had brought to his bedside just before he fell asleep. Had he drunk it, he would have been just now deaf to the witches'

glee. He heard and saw them drink health in such a mocking style as nearly to tempt him to charge them, besom in hand, but he restrained himself.

The jug being emptied, one of them cried out, 'Is it time to be gone?' and at the same moment, putting on a red cap, she added –

> 'By yarrow and rue,
> And my red cap too,
> Hie over to England.'

Making use of a twig which she held in her hand as a steed, she gracefully soared up the chimney, and was rapidly followed by the rest. But when it came to the housekeeper, Shemus interposed. 'By your leave, ma'am,' said he, snatching twig and cap. 'Ah, you desateful ould crocodile! If I find you here on my return, there'll be wigs on the green –

120

"By yarrow and rue,
And my red cap too,
Hie over to England".'

The words were not out of his mouth when he was soaring above the ridge pole, and swiftly ploughing the air. He was careful to speak no word (being somewhat conversant with witch-lore), as the result would be a tumble, and the immediate return of the expedition.

In a very short time they had crossed the Wicklow hills, the Irish Sea, and the Welsh mountains, and were charging, at whirlwind speed, the hall door of a castle. Shemus, only for the company in which he found himself, would have cried out for pardon, expecting to be *mummy* against the hard oak door in a moment; but, all bewildered, he found himself passing through the keyhole, along a passage, down a flight of steps, and through a cellar-door key-hole before he could form any clear idea of his situation.

Waking to the full consciousness of his position, he found himself sitting on a stillion, plenty of lights

glimmering round, and he and his companions, with full tumblers of frothing wine in hand, hob-nobbing and drinking healths as jovially and recklessly as if the liquor was honestly come by, and they were sitting in *Shemus's* own kitchen. The red birredh (cap) had assimilated *Shemus's* nature for the time being to that of his unholy companions.

(*Facing page*) Witches and devils cavorting – a picture by Edward Zier (1885). (*Above*) Members of the 'Devil's Legion' prepare to leave for the Sabbat: a picture by John D. Batten for the story 'The Horned Women' from *Celtic Fairy Tales*. (*Below*) Another magnificent engraving by Gustave Doré entitled 'Flight of the Witches' (1875).

121

The heady liquors soon got into their brains, and a period of unconsciousness succeeded the ecstasy, the head-ache, the turning round of the barrels, and the 'scattered sight' of poor Shemus. He woke up under the impression of being roughly seized, and shaken, and dragged upstairs, and subjected to a disagreeable examination by the lord of the castle, in his state parlour. There was much derision among the whole company, gentle and simple, on hearing Shemus's explanation, and, as the thing occurred in the dark ages, the unlucky Leinster man was sentenced to be hung as soon as the gallows could be prepared.

The poor Hibernian was in the cart proceeding on his last journey, with a label on his back, and another on his breast, announcing him as the remorseless villain who for the last month had been draining the casks in my lord's vault every night. He was surprised to hear himself addressed by his name, and in his native tongue, by an old woman in the crowd. 'Ach, Shemus, alanna! is it going to die you are in a strange place without your *cappeen d'yarrag*?' (red cap). These words infused hope and courage into the poor victim's heart. He turned to the lord and humbly asked leave to die in his red cap, which he supposed had dropped from his head in the vault. A servant was sent for the head-piece, and Shemus felt lively hope warming his heart while placing it on his head. On the platform he was graciously allowed to address the spectators, which he proceeded to do in the usual formula composed for the benefit of flying stationers – 'Good people all, a warning take by me'; but when he had finished the line, 'My parents reared me tenderly,' he unexpectedly added – 'By yarrow and rue,' etc., and the disappointed spectators saw him shoot up obliquely through the air in the style of a sky-rocket that had missed its aim. It is said that the lord took the circumstance much to heart, and never afterwards hung a man for twenty-four hours after his offence.

(*Above*) An old witch as visualised by Arthur Rackham for *Irish Fairy Tales*. (*Facing page*) 'The Hand of Glory' drawn by Michael Ayrton for *Ghosts and Witches* (1954).

The Fantasy Land of Lord Dunsany

No book about the Irish supernatural could possibly be complete without a section on Lord Dunsany, the Irish peer who 'fathered' the invented fantasy world in short story form. For in a way his work took all the elements that have been described and illustrated in the pages of this book and turned them into a special kind of story.

Though tales of wonder have been a part of literature for centuries, Lord Dunsany was the man who created the short fantasy story which is now so popular, and to a large extent as a result of this has become widely regarded as the greatest writer of fantasy literature. There is certainly no denying his works have been a favourite with readers of several generations and an influence on almost all writers in the genre.

The fantasy land which he writes about is timeless and has no set location, although it deals with a variety of ancient gods and exotic people and places. Yet there is something of Ireland in it, too. Indeed it is possible to see through these stories that the author was a man deeply influenced by the local legends he grew up with and which were part of his heritage, and how he used these with his remarkable imagination to produce such outstanding works as *The Gods of Pegana* (1905), *Time and the Gods* (1906), *The Sword of Welleran* (1908), *A Dreamer's Tales* (1910) and *Tales of Wonder* (1916) as well as over fifty other volumes of novels, short stories, plays and poetry.

Lord Dunsany (1878–1957), the 18th Baron Dunsany, was as remarkable a man as his books: big game hunter, war hero, P. O. W. escaper, chess champion and bon viveur. He could write light-hearted fantasy just as easily as tales of chilling evil, and he was certainly fortunate in the development of his popularity in having his books illustrated by one of the finest imaginative artists of the day, Sidney H. Sime. A selection of his drawings from some of Dunsany's best fantasy titles makes a most fitting way of closing this survey of the Irish worlds of wonder, I believe.

WORLDS OF WONDER

Three of Sidney H. Sime's marvellous drawings for Lord Dunsany's *The Gods of Pegana*. (*Facing page*) The Land of Pegana. (*Left*) 'It' and (*Above*) 'Mung and the Beast of Mung'.

(*Above, left*) 'The Soul of
Andelsprutz' from *A Dreamer's Tales*.
(*Above, right*) 'Lo! The Gods' from
Time and the Gods; and (*Right*)
'Welleran And The Sword of
Welleran.' from *The Sword of
Welleran*. (*Facing page*) Perhaps the
finest and most evocative of all
Sidney Sime's illustrations for
Dunsany's books also taken from *The
Sword of Welleran*.

ACKNOWLEDGEMENTS

The author is grateful to numerous people in both England and Ireland for supplying books and illustrations for use in the compiling of this work, but would like to thank the following in particular: Ken Chapman, Nina Rigden, George Locke; the staffs of the British Museum, The London Library and the Harry Price Library; Holden Books, Clark Publishing Co, *The Occult Review*, *The Daily Express*, and The Hutchinson Publishing Group for 'The Jack O'Lanterns' by Lord Dunsany. Also the representatives of Michael Ayrton, Arthur Rackham, W. Heath Robinson and Rowel Friers. While every care has been taken in establishing copyright in material used in this book, in case of any accidental infringement please write to the author in care of the publishers.